D. B McLachlan

Reformed Logic

A System Based on Berkeley's Philosophy with an Entirely New Method of Dialectic

D. B McLachlan

Reformed Logic
A System Based on Berkeley's Philosophy with an Entirely New Method of Dialectic

ISBN/EAN: 9783337077488

Printed in Europe, USA, Canada, Australia, Japan

Cover: Foto ©Thomas Meinert / pixelio.de

More available books at **www.hansebooks.com**

REFORMED LOGIC

A SYSTEM BASED ON

BERKELEY'S PHILOSOPHY

WITH AN ENTIRELY NEW METHOD OF

DIALECTIC

BY

D. B. McLACHLAN

'SPIRITS are active, indivisible substances; IDEAS [objects] are inert, fleeting, dependent things, which subsist not by themselves, but are supported by, or exist in minds or spiritual substances . . . The cause of Ideas is an incorporeal active SUBSTANCE or Spirit.'
—*Berkeley.*

London
SWAN SONNENSCHEIN & CO
PATERNOSTER SQUARE
1892

[*All rights reserved*]

'*Looking to the chaotic state of logic text-books at the present time,* one would be inclined to say that there does not exist *anywhere a recognised, currently-received body of speculation* to which the title Logic can be unambiguously assigned, and that we must therefore resign the hope of attaining by any empirical consideration of the received doctrine, a precise determination of the nature and limits of logical theory.'

Encyc. **Brit.,** Art. Logic.

PREFACE

The object of the following treatise is to give an intelligible account of the principal facts of Mind, with a method for the right expression and criticism of Reasoning. It is based on principles not before applied to such a purpose. The current systems of Metaphysic are obscure and difficult simply because they start from false premises, not because the nature and operations of Mind cannot, if properly understood, be made as comprehensible to beginners as other branches of knowledge. The rules of Dialectic are quite within the capacity of any intelligent schoolboy, and should be an essential part of early education, like Arithmetic.

Let not the student be repelled at finding a philosophy reputed to be one of the most difficult taken as the basis of this work. It is Berkeleyism considerably modified. Also it is to be borne in mind that a philosophy is not to be judged by its *primâ facie* probability, but by its power of explaining many facts in a coherent and lucid way. A theory that does this should not be rejected for a seeming paradox at the outset.

Most of the theoretical and all the dialectical parts of this work can be adapted to Realistic thinking, by treating the judgments of the two Berkeleyan categories as intuitions instead of inferences.

CONTENTS

	PAGE
PREFACE	v

INTRODUCTION

SECT.
I   Division of Philosophies into Ideal and Substantial—Substantial subdivided into Mental and Material—Berkeley's philosophy a Mental Substantialism   1

II Ontological principles essential to logical theory—Mind consists of (at least) Self and a Plastic Substance—Functions of each—Perception of Inorganic things discussed—Berkeley's view on this point rejected—Body to be considered an apparatus of Perception . . .   4

III Current Metaphysic is Ideal and therefore incoherent—Substantial alone has a connecting principle—Importance of Categories in Substantialism—Its doctrine of Reason totally different from the Academic   8

INTELLECT

IV Origin of Intellect—Its use—Difference between Sentimental and Intellectual consciousness—Intellect not the governing intelligence of Man—Moral education the most important   11

V   Truth, its various meanings—Veracity—Correct Ideation—Correct Inference—No absolute standard of Truth—*Nisi utile est, quod novimus, stulta est Sapientia*—Schopenhauer on the function of Intellect   14

SECT.		PAGE
VI	Standard of Truth relating to Bodily welfare different from that relating to Mental welfare—Realism the theory of Perception under the former standard—Its main dogmas—Cause why it is superseded—Superstition of One Truth—Realism and Substantialism both true and yet contradictory	18

PERCEPTION

| VII | Defined, according to Substantial principles—Noumenon—Subject—Object—Sentiment not excited by Objects, but Objects accompany Sentiments—Subject not passive in Perception—ATTENTION—Kant's opinion on the inconceivability of Noumena refuted—Difficulty of overcoming Realistic prejudices—Science of little use in Philosophy . | 23 |

IDEAS

VIII	How produced—Hume's notion untenable—No innate Ideas—but Sentiment is innate—Division of Ideas into Particular, General, and Imaginary	27
IX	MEMORY—OBLIVION—RECOLLECTION—Images, how preserved and how lost—Good Memory not necessarily advantageous—Recovery of the apparently Forgotten—Sudden extinction of Ideas—'Decay of the mind' in old age—Memory inexplicable on any theory but the Substantial—John Stuart Mill's confession—Memory the chief fact of Mental Science	28
X	Sentiments may be remembered—Feelings and Emotions—No detailed analysis of Sentiments possible or necessary—Spinoza's list—Can sentiments be noumenally excited without objects?	34
XI	Analysis of Comparison—It is the principle of Generalisation and Imagination	36

✝ GENERALISATION

| XII | Purpose of Generalisation—Objects classified must be similar and have similar utilities—Inferiority of general |

SECT.		PAGE
	ideas acquired **by definition—Names not essential to general** thought—Generalisation resembles composite photography—Classification **on** mere objective resemblance—neat but superficial—Conceptualism	38
XIII	MATTER the most general **notion derived from Objects**—Belief in Real Matter **a form of Mysticism—A material** basis for phenomena **unnecessary**	43
XIV	NOMINALISM—Berkeley's Nominalism, **and objections thereto—Concrete Thought expressed in general terms**	46
XV	Generalisation the bane of **European** philosophy—Plato's theories on General Ideas—Aristotle's 'Essence'—Classification a means, not the end of Reason—The explanatory Unity a unity of service—Evolution a concrete Platonism	58

IMAGINATION

| XVI | How distinguished from Recollection and Reverie—Imagination by Simple Combination—By Transfusion—Artistic Imagination—Rational Imagination—Wrong views of Metaphysicians | 63 |

DIALECTIC

XVII	Recapitulation of the genealogy of Reason—It is the art of conceiving the Future and Unknown—Dialectic the science of Reason—Division of theorems into Arguments and Fallacies—Method of Dialectic	68
XVIII	The RATIONAL PARALLEL—Rational Conclusions are never certain—Essential parts of an Argument—Rules of Parallel—False conclusions cannot be destroyed but may be stigmatised—In what circumstances we may reason concerning a known fact	74
XIX	Hypothetical Arguments—Current errors with respect to these—Dilemma	80
XX	DEBATE is extra-dialectic—How a valid argument may be criticised	87

Categories

SECT.		PAGE
XXI	Natural— Realistic — Scientific—Philosophical—Categories of Pythagoreans—of Aristotle—of Kant, etc.	92
XXII	Category of Inherence—It is a metaphysical analysis of objects—Examples of Judgment and Argument—Use of Standards for Mediate Comparison	97
XXIII	Category of Association defined—Position—Examples of Judgment and Argument—Movement—Number—Flat Space	103
XXIV	Perspection or Depth in groups—Perspective degradation—Redintegration, real and ideal—This groupment as a fixed Precedent—Standard of Depth—Sky Perspection	108
XXV	Concretion of Cubic ideas from flat objects—Backs of things—Resistance—Dr. Johnson on Idealism—Danger of trifling with Idealists, illustrated from the Dabistán—Geographical Concretion—Its superiority to mere Recollection—Sphericity of the Earth, what it means	118
XXVI	Material Sequence defined, with examples—TIME the interval between objects in Sequence—Eternity—Scientific confusion of Sequence with Causation	126
XXVII	CAUSATION—Its peculiarities—How distinguished from Sequence—Effects are never causes—Cause consists of Motive, Plan, and Power—Generation not causation—Atoms not causes—Sub-categories of Causation—'Conservation' of Energy discussed — Note on DREAMS	130

Redaction of Colloquial Arguments

XXVIII	Language not naturally an instrument of Argument—How to adapt it to this purpose—Negative words—Partitive words—Redaction does not extend to the correction of faulty observation—Syllogistic Conversion not necessary on the Substantial method	151

Fallacies

SECT.		PAGE
XXIX	Of Equivocation—Of Imperfect Observation	157
XXX	Of Parallel Arrangement — Suppressed Precedent — Inferring a negative from Contrast—False Analogy — Doubtful Precedent—Of Accident—Of Division —Of Composition — Dialectical Tautology — Cross Reasoning — Fallacy of No Case — Of Inversion— Suppressed Conclusion — Of No Application — Of Irrelevant Conclusion	161

Academical Dialectic.

XXXI	Various notions of Reason entertained by Syllogists —One only true, Analogy	175
XXXII	'Immediate Inference' is not Argument, but explicitness and emphasis in language	176
XXXIII	Arithmetic, what it is—The Real and the Symbolic— Reasoning enters only into the Real—The Symbolic a kind of expression	177
XXXIV	Geometrical Demonstration not a form of Reasoning —The so-called 'deductive reasoning' of Geometry a graduated series of lessons in perception	182
XXXV	Induction not a special kind of reasoning, but a deduction with suppressed precedent—Other meanings of the word	185
XXXVI	Aristotle's Dictum explained and refuted	187
XXXVII	Mediate Comparison not Argument	189
XXXVIII	Syllogism analysed—It is not Argument—Doctrine of the Predicate—Moods of the Syllogism discussed —All moods reducible to One	191

Studies in Dialectic

XXXIX	Additional examples to illustrate the Dialectic of Substantialism	205

INTRODUCTION

I—RELATION OF BERKELEY'S PHILOSOPHY TO OTHER SYSTEMS

PHILOSOPHIES are either Ideal or Substantial. The ideal are those which resolve all things, actual and possible, into thought or consciousness. They seek to find in consciousness the reason and meaning of itself, or, if this be impossible, to account for each item in consciousness by defining its relation to some other item, or to some general mass of consciousness. This type of philosophy includes German transcendentalism and idealism, and some species of Buddhist and Persian metaphysic. European idealists are seldom consistent, for at the basis of their philosophies (or at the apex) they place GOD, who is not an item of human consciousness, actual or potential, and who therefore occupies, whether it be admitted or not, the relation of substance to human thought.

Substantial philosophies affirm that thought invariably inheres in some sort of Substance, for whose service it exists. It is incapable of independent being, and cannot be understood abstracted from its substance. It is intermittent, called up when wanted, and is liable to variation and aberration.

Substantialists differ however as to what the substance of human intelligence is. Some hold that it is the human body. Consciousness exists, they argue, for the use of the body and varies with its condition. This class of philosophers may be subdivided into Materialists and Metaphysicians (including logicians).

Materialists believe that consciousness is a product of the physical body—has therefore no existence before the body is formed or after it is dissolved. It is really as physical as the teeth or hair.

In metaphysic the intelligence is supposed to have a principle of existence apart from the body, and does not, or need not, share the fate of the body. The body is nevertheless regarded as the substance or superior fact during the union of the two. This is an eminently inconsistent philosophy, for if consciousness has an existence apart from body it must be in some other substance, and if so its relations to that substance are more important than its relations to the body, and should be the first object of inquiry. Metaphysic is in its development an idealism, since the connection admitted between body and thought is too slight to afford a sufficient explanation of intelligence, and no other substantial relation is known.

The notion that an invisible immaterial substance may underlie consciousness has occurred to some philosophers, among others to the illustrious BERKELEY. His theory of Vision, which has never been refuted or even weakened, is founded on this hypothesis.

Berkeleyan substantialism combines the characteristic features of the other theories, and affords an easy solution of many difficult problems in philosophy. It has in common with idealism—whence it is sometimes, but erroneously, called by that name—that it regards all *material* bodies and things as facts or items of consciousness. It agrees with materialism that a substance is essential to consciousness, and that the consciousness of man serves the needs of his body, though that is not the highest use to which it can be put. It confirms the metaphysical view that intelligence is not, in its abstract or essential character, dependent on the body, and may therefore survive the body.

This is the theory on which the following logic is based : I shall refer to it briefly as Substantialism.

II—ONTOLOGICAL NOTIONS

SUBSTANTIALISM has two main divisions—Ontology, which treats of the mental substance in itself, and Logic or Metaphysic, which deals with its consciousness. The present essay is specially concerned with logic, but certain ontological premises must be assumed to render the logic intelligible. This follows from the subordinate relation of consciousness to substance.

The substantial mind consists of two principal parts—a SELF and a PLASMA—the Atman and Akaśa of Sanscrit philosophers.

Self is the seat of Energy and Consciousness. The plasma is inert and unconscious; it protects the Self and receives, communicates, and retains impressions of experience, both the external and the internal[1].

[1] The mental substance is the *fifth essence* of the initiate Greeks and of Alchemists. They also called it *chaos* and *first matter*. 'Man was made of that very matter and chaos whereof all the world was made, and all the creatures in it: which is a most high mystery to understand, and must, nay is altogether necessary to be known of him that expecteth good from this art, being the ground of the wisdom thereof. Foolish men, nay they that the world holds for great doctors, say and tell it for truth, that God made man of a piece of mud, or clay, or dust of the earth, which is false; it was no such matter, but a Quintessential Matter which is called earth, but is no earth.'—*De Manna Benedicto.*

The Self would be conscious though isolated from other minds, at least from those of its own grade of being. It would feel the fluctuations of its energy. But the experience called 'external' depends on the mutual action of minds. It is the form into which their consciousness is thrown when they come in contact. It lasts no longer than the contact, and so has only a casual existence.

The constitution of the mind is not given by Berkeley, and on other points also we must supplement and correct his philosophy. He was wrong as regards the mental cause of the perception of the Inorganic or Dead.

Since external experience implies that another mind is operating upon ours, what mind is operating when we perceive an object that is apparently mindless? Berkeley replies that it is the supreme mind that is then acting upon us.

Many objections can be urged against this view. I will mention only one, which seems to me conclusive. By every canon of judgment we possess, the living or organised is better—more important and significant—than the lifeless and elemental; so if Berkeley's reasoning be valid the phenomena excited by finite and created beings are superior to those excited by their Creator. The movements of a living man are referred to a human mind—a putrescent carcase is a vision immediately induced by the Deity.

The beauty of the starry sky is irrelevant to the question. Apart from the finite life and thought that may be associated with the stars, they have no more philosophical importance than a spadeful of sand.

A more reasonable account of the inorganic is found in several ancient philosophies. Gnostics and Neo-Platonists referred the elemental to a cosmic mind (*Demiurgos*) intermediate between human beings and the Supreme. The demiurgic mind is inconceivably greater and more powerful than the human, but is not necessarily better in quality. It is the origin of all natural forces, and its organic processes are what we term 'physical laws.' This is the explanation of inorganic consciousness which I feel disposed to adopt, but to discuss it fully would carry us too far from the subject of this work.

The next point relates to the body. What is its function in substantialism? The brain, says Berkeley, is an idea in the mind, and he ridicules the notion that one idea should generate all other ideas. This is an argument against materialism. No doubt he would have admitted, though he does not say so, that the body-idea facilitates, or at least must precede, the experience of other ideas. He would not have denied that it is an *instrumental* idea.

Since his time an important discovery has been made with reference to the constitution of the body. I allude to the Cell theory. It is no longer possible to regard the body either as a self-moving machine (if this is not a contradiction in terms), or as a lump of 'dead matter' animated by the mind. It is a society of minute animals[1], each having a certain degree of independent energy and liberty of movement. They are organised and governed by the human or animal mind with which they are associated. In short, the relation of the cell to the man is analogous to, if not quite the same as, the relation of the man to the cosmic being.

This discovery complicates the problem of 'external' consciousness, without however affecting the principles on which a substantialist would endeavour to solve it. Instead of conceiving human minds as coming into immediate contact in perception, we have to conceive the cellular systems of each as forming a medium between the two. We do not perceive the other mind immediately or intuitively; what we perceive intuitively is certain affections in our own organism, which we must first refer to the other body, and then to the mind behind that body. Our knowledge of other human beings is thus altogether inferential.

The cellular medium explains why we are not generally aware of the substantial constitution of other minds; it is veiled by the intervening organisms.

---

[1] See Stricker's *Manual of Histology*; *Bioplasm*, and other works, by Dr Lionel S. Beale, M.B., F.R.S.; and an article on the New Psychology, by A. Fouillé, in the *Revue des Deux Mondes* for October 15th, 1891.

The relation of body to mind, the reason of embodiment, and so forth, are questions of prime importance in ontology, but in logic we are concerned only with the object in consciousness, without reference to the apparatus of perception. The instrument of intellectual perception may in its proper character be ignored.

III—DIFFERENCES BETWEEN SUBSTANTIAL AND METAPHYSICAL LOGIC

ALL the current academic metaphysic is ideal. Materialists, when they attempt to explain thought, fail to attach it properly to the body, or to account for that large and important division of mental activity which has no bearing, direct or indirect, on bodily welfare. They drop their materialism at an early stage of their enquiry and continue on the metaphysical method.

Hence in none of the current systems is there any true principle of arrangement in the treatment of logical phenomena. Unless we know the use of a thing we cannot describe it, let alone explain it. We know not the relative importance of its parts, and we arrange them according to superficial resemblances, or on some arbitrary principle which conceals instead of revealing their meaning.

Substantial philosophy alone possesses a principle of coherence. The facts of consciousness are determined by anterior facts of substance, and there can be only one true mode in which to present them—they must follow and reflect the substantial order. They will thus appear as a consecutive and coherent system of ideas, no one of which could be otherwise placed without damage to the whole. This is perhaps the most important respect in which substantial logic differs from others.

The doctrine of Categories has to receive full development in order to elucidate the genesis of the 'material world.' Except to a substantialist the categories have no particular value, and so they are barely mentioned in the academic systems.

The theory of Reasoning or Dialectic (logic in the narrower sense) given in the following chapters, will be found totally different from the academic. It does not merely state in other words or metaphors the doctrines laid down in works of the Aristotelian type,—it declares that the theory of reasoning taught in these works is altogether false. Our argumentation is not conducted in syllogisms, either tacit or explicit. This has been suspected by several critics of logic, but no attempt has been made to substitute a more correct theory and method.

Of course logicians do not always reason wrongly, and true arguments may be stated in the syllogistic form. What I mean is that logicians nowhere tell us in what right reasoning essentially consists, and for want of a distinct notion on the subject they all of them occasionally admit as valid, arguments that are not so.

The main dogma of substantialism should be kept in view in reading the following pages. It is mind alone that is conceived as having solidity and energy: material things are temporary forms of our consciousness; they have length and breadth but no depth, and they are without energy, even passive resistance. If an object cannot be removed at pleasure, what resists us is the other mind causing that object, not the object itself.

As far as possible I have utilised the existing logical terminology. But substantialism has notions which require special technical words, and I have not hesitated to invent such when necessary. On the other hand, I have rejected the latinisms of current logic, which have never been assimilated by modern languages. The English language is good enough for all the purposes of logic.

INTELLECT

IV—ITS ORIGIN AND FUNCTION

THE mind has at physical birth one uniform quality of plasma and consciousness. By education and experience a portion of the plasma is gradually changed, and the consciousness excited by this portion is what we call INTELLECT. The word may also stand for the plasma so differentiated.

The consciousness pertaining to the plasma left in its primitive state is SENTIMENT, which generally corresponds to what is termed the moral nature of man.

Intellect is a temporary condition arising out of the need to preserve the Self from hostile and inharmonious surroundings. The adaptation is artificial, and may therefore be well-done, or ill-done, or over-done.

It is over-done when too much of the plasma and mental energy is devoted to intellectual purposes—when the individual has, to use a common expression, more head than heart. In this case the end is sacrificed to the means.

I conceive the intellect as a hardening of the plasma in its superficies, the formation of a sort of rind capable of receiving finer, sharper, and more enduring impressions than the plasma of sentiment; and, being harder, it is better able than the latter to resist enfeebling influences. Its duty is to challenge and inspect vibrations before permitting them to pass inwards to the region of sentiment. Yet the intellectual consciousness is itself a degree of sentiment, and in intellects not sufficiently trained it may be impossible to distinguish thoughts that are purely intellectual, from thoughts that are also to some extent sentimental. Upon minds of this sort the best-prepared arguments have no hold; they must be mixed with oratory and poetry to receive any attention. It need not be said that a mind which responds only to 'persuasive' language is feeble of intellect. It lives in the present only, and is incapable of far-reaching designs. It is to the intellect we owe the power of conceiving the past and future, and of laying plans for the future.

A mind properly intellectualised is, of its kind, strong and self-controlled. With the intellect defective the man exhibits passion, undue excitement and demonstrativeness. He responds to the least stimulus, like an exposed nerve; his energy is wasted in explosions. Sentiment is the inmost nerve of man— intellect its protecting sheath. The most carefully trained intellect is liable at times to be carried by assault or stratagem; then follows a feeling of emptiness occasioned by loss of energy. On the other hand an appearance of self-command may be really due to apathy,—the mind is of a low type and callous to influences that usually affect its species. If it is bad to be explosive, it is perhaps worse to be incapable of exploding.

Intellect is not the supreme or ruling intelligence of man. It initiates nothing. It is a light to direct our steps, but we do not walk where the light happens to fall—we make it fall where we desire to walk. Hence the diversity of occupation and intellectual accomplishments in men. Each acquires the sort of intellect he thinks will be sentimentally most serviceable to him; and on matters concerning which he has not learnt to reason he consults other men. We are not born rational beings; we are in no sense rational on all subjects; we are rational only on those few which we have mastered.

Men pretend to act from reason only, and perhaps they do on matters to which they are indifferent. But in general their rationality consists in finding pretexts for what on sentimental grounds they have already resolved to do, and in finding ways and means to carry out their resolves. Sentiment is the moving spring of conduct: intellect is the executive faculty. Those historical philosophers are mistaken who suppose the progress of mankind results from intellectual discoveries and inventions. These are effects, not causes, of progress—effects of *sentimental* disagreement with previous conditions.

Intellect is little more than an extension inwards of our senses. It is an epitome and rearrangement of their observations, and is as instrumental as they. We are not necessarily improved by a development of the intellect forced upon us from without. Education is sometimes a dagger put into the hands of an assassin. The best education is largely sentimental (moral), for that is not confined to preserving the mind we have—it gives us another and a better mind, and so indirectly improves the intellect.

V—TRUTH

THIS word has several meanings which it may be well to notice.

As *veracity* it means an agreement between our thoughts and our language. It supposes that we take reasonable pains to learn the conventional laws upon which language is founded, and then endeavour as far as possible to bring our speech in conformity with these laws. Since language is an art (like music) it may be acquired well or ill, so that a mistake in the use of a phrase or term is not regarded as untruth. There must be deliberate abuse of language to constitute a lie.

Agreement between an idea of memory and the actual experience—correct recollection—is another meaning of truth.

Also truth may signify agreement between an inferential thought and the fact to which it refers, although the fact has not yet been observed. In this sense truth must be construed liberally. We never foresee a future fact exactly as it will take place. Our anticipations are vague and our preparations for them general, but that on the whole is enough for our purposes. At least it is all that reason affords us. If we are absolutely certain of a future fact and can figure it in the mind precisely as it will take place, that means that it has already occurred so often that we are virtually using our memory, not our reason.

An inference may be considered true if it is the best we can draw from the information at our command, though in point of fact it may prove to be very incorrect.

There is no mass of speculative Truth which everybody ought to possess on pain of being considered foolish or miscreant. This notion, formerly so prevalent, betrays gross ignorance of the nature and function of intellect. It makes intellectual speculation an end in itself. Our ideas must be such as serve the uses of our sentimental or inner soul, and since the sentiments (tastes) of men vary widely, so ought also their intellectual ideas. Though change of sentiment modifies ideas, change of ideas does not modify sentiment. There is therefore no sort of good in uniformity of belief in itself. It is creditable to modern times that men have shaken off the procrustean beliefs of the Middle Ages, and are free to adapt their intellects to their real sentimental needs. The numerous sections into which speculative thought is now broken up, and the frequent changes of theory, are signs of healthy and active sentiment.

In matters of social policy, where large bodies of men have to carry out a single design, uniformity must be attained by persuasion or compromise. But such matters relate only to physical well-being, into which philosophical truth can hardly be said to enter.

This relative and, in the widest sense, utilitarian view of intellectual truth applies both to quantity and quality of ideas. We should not learn what we do not sentimentally require. That is waste of power. Useless knowledge is folly, said both Plato and Aristotle. To mistake knowledge to be the pursuit of man is to confuse the means with the end, says the author of the Bhagavad Gita.

The quality of our ideas must not be good beyond our necessities. If they are, we shall suffer by acting on them. They will land us in circumstances for which our nature is not fully prepared.

If there were an abstract or standard truth, it would be good for every species of being, and no doubt the thoughts of a man are nearer to it than the thoughts of a horse. Therefore a horse ought to be improved by receiving a human intellect. But if we could insinuate into a horse's mind the knowledge possessed by an educated man, we should spoil what may have been a good horse and produce a monstrous and horrible man. So is it with ourselves. If we could receive knowledge far in advance of our requirements or out of relation to them, it would drive us mad or be itself madness. Our constitution and necessities determine what we can know and what we ought to know. Not all possible knowledge is good, and what is good for some may be useless or bad for others. Schopenhauer says well[1]: 'The faculty of Knowing .... has only arisen for the purpose of self-preservation, and therefore stands in a precise relation, admitting of countless gradations, to the requirements of each animal species.'

[1] *Will in Nature,* 'Physiology of Plants.'

VI—REALISM

If our interests were single and uniform, one consistent scheme of intellectual knowledge would suffice. We need never be in fundamental contradiction with ourselves. Every advance in knowledge would illustrate and confirm what we had already learned.

But we are not of this simple constitution. We are first and essentially minds, we are next and temporarily embodied minds, and in each of these characters we have distinct and, to a great extent, conflicting interests. Hence we have to acquire different species of knowledge and admit different standards of truth. The ideas that serve the interests of the embodied man are false to the same man considered apart from his embodiment, and contrariwise—false, in the sense of being useless and perhaps misleading.

Hence the existence of Common-sense for the embodied interests, and Philosophy for the purely mental interests. Science is common knowledge carried to its utmost perfection, but not partaking in the least of the philosophical character.

Realism is the notion of perception that is acquired with our common knowledge. It is seldom explicitly defined or defended, for in order to this a comparison with philosophic theories would have to be made, and the defects of realism would be apparent. The realistic view is so named by philosophers to distinguish it from their own views.

For corporeal purposes it is useful to believe, and it is therefore relatively true, that there is a real space which would exist although all objects were removed from it. Objects are real solid things stored in space like casks in a cellar. They have fixed dimensions notwithstanding that they appear to contract and dilate as we leave or approach them. It is quite 'natural' they should appear smaller at a distance. Distant perception is conceivable, therefore it is possible, and since calculations based on this assumption are verified by experience, it must and does take place. Time also is as real as space, and would exist by itself though space and its contents were annihilated. It is a sort of stream.

All these propositions are true for certain necessary purposes. We begin to form such ideas from the moment we are born, and during the years of infancy we are doing nothing else intellectually but working out the notions of space, time, magnitude, distance. Most of our school education is of the same kind. By the time we reach maturity realism has become so rooted in our intellect that—as regards the majority of men—no sceptical considerations are strong enough to unsettle them. For why? They enable the natural man to provide sufficiently well for his bodily needs and other needs depending therefrom, and he has therefore no motive for doubting his realism or for acquiring any other sort of ideas. He is quite right to abide by those which have answered his purposes.

It is not from without but from within that doubts arise as to realistic truth. They arise when the mind has acquired power over and above what is needed for bodily uses, and begins to think on its own account. Sentiments are felt which do not depend on or refer to bodily life, and a new intellect has to be formed to explain and protect these sentiments. This new intellect is Philosophy. It is the science and practical conduct of mind considered as abstracted from body.

Much of the obscurity of philosophy is traceable to the superstition of a fixed standard of truth which must be recognised universally. We are reluctant to accept philosophical hints and inferences because they conflict with truths that have been physically verified. Or—which is more common—we take up a few philosophical propositions and tack on to them all the science we know, believing they make a homogeneous whole, because truth must be self-consistent.

Time and labour would be spared if we could be told at the right moment that truth is expedience[1],

---

[1] This does not apply to truth in the sense of veracity.

and that there is no need to harmonise philosophy and science. We are each of us two men in one, and each of these men must be allowed to think for himself. There is no reason why they should quarrel; there is no reason why they should even argue. The science in our mind should not be ousted to make room for the philosophy; let them exist together and work alternately. When the mariner is at sea he must mind his ship and study the weather; when he is on shore he may neglect both. So when we are navigating the body we have to think in categories proper to its safety; as philosophers we dismiss the realistic categories and think in other forms, but we need not then call the realism false or foolish. In its proper place it is right and true[1].

Between realism and substantialism there is therefore no necessary conflict or competition. They are each indispensable. It is absurd to carry realism into philosophy, and no less absurd to carry substantialism

[1] Greek philosophers never understood the dual standard of Truth, and insisted that philosophy was the best preparation for every sort of employment. The people, though generally unwise in political matters, had sense enough not to entrust the care of their temporal interests to philosophers, and so the universal utility of philosophy had few opportunities of being tested. A Macedonian king committed the custody of Corinth and its citadel to a philosopher, Persaeus, who was promptly expelled by Aratus—a mere soldier. Persaeus frequented the schools again, and on the well-worn theme that 'none but a wise man is fit to be a general' being brought up for discussion, he said, 'It is true, and the gods know it, that this maxim of Zeno once pleased me more than all the rest; but I have changed my opinion since I was taught better by the young Sicyonian.'—Plutarch's *Life of Aratus*.

into common affairs, or to reproach a substantialist because he acts and speaks occasionally like other people. It is probable however that in a community largely composed of substantialists the realism of common action would be less stringent than is now found necessary.

PERCEPTION

VII

PERCEPTION has already been partially defined. So-called 'external objects' are forms excited in our consciousness by pressure of other minds. The great permanent 'world' is due to the action of a cosmic mind with which we are intimately associated throughout our physical life.

Objects have a totally different sort of existence from minds, for whereas the latter are—at least relative to objects—self-existent, the former have no existence except during the act of perception. If minds could be all moved asunder from each other the whole objective world would disappear, yet the universe would be as full as before, for sensation occupies no room.

The appearances we interpret as distance are due to variations in the pressure or stimulus producing the object.

It will be convenient to call the more active mind *Noumenon*, the perceiving mind *Subject*. The mind that is subject on one occasion may be noumenon at another, and conversely. The true antithesis to subject is not object, but noumenon. Object has no antithesis, unless it be nonentity.

It is specially to be noticed that an object is not the *cause* of a sentiment. The knife we see or handle is not the cause of the pain it may inflict if driven into our flesh. Pains and pleasures signify that the noumenal action is powerful enough not only to excite objects in the intellect, but to penetrate inwards and excite sentiments also. It is the noumenon that causes both object and sentiment, as far as the energy exerted is concerned, but the variation of plasma in the subject is also essential to the distinction of object and sentiment.

The subject is not quite passive in perception. No consciousness takes place unless the subject is charged with energy. Further, since consciousness is confined to the Self and not inherent in the plasma, we perceive only such vibrations as reach the Self. If the Self is absorbed in one part of the mind, vibrations may take place in other parts without being noticed. The more energy we concentrate at the point or surface of contact (Attention), or otherwise bring to bear on the plasmic vibration, the more vivid is the object.

The fixing or circumscribing of attention so as to break up our experience into distinct things or objects is an acquired art, whence we may infer that the intellectual experience of infancy is a vague whitish surface, not clearly distinguished by colour or movement.

Kant and other philosophers admit that objects are caused by noumena, but insist that we can never know or conceive what a noumenon is.

Why not? Each of us knows himself to be the noumenon of many phenomena; he has no doubt that many other phenomena are caused by minds like himself, and it is easy to extend this principle to all phenomena whatever. They are all caused by minds more or less like human minds. This is a useful conclusion, although we are not able to imagine very accurately the mind of an insect or of a being of cosmic dimensions. It is not necessary we should, but the most general inference of this sort is better than none at all, and better than the notion that phenomena are self-existent and self-moving.

Although simple and intelligible when stated in the abstract, perception is difficult to work out in detail. Objections start up on every side, and it requires the utmost patience to reduce them to what they are—*inferences* from the realism we are supposed to have discarded. It is only when we try to dislodge realism wholly and consistently that we find how fast its hold upon our intellect is. Critics who profess to treat Berkeley's substantialism seriously and sympathetically, constantly bring up against it arguments of the most naively realistic kind. They have no adequate conception how enormous is the revolution in thought involved in substituting substantialism for realism. It is a complete dissolution of the natural thought and belief; it means the construction of a new heaven and a new earth with laws to which we have been hitherto unaccustomed. The old science is of little or no use to us as substantialists.

Philosophy is not an advance or correction of science. In so far as the latter claims to be absolutely or philosophically true, substantialism abolishes it in dispensing with the notions of real matter and real space. Hence it is quite irrelevant to point out that substantialism is inconsistent with (say) the doctrine of physical evolution. This theory, though so new, is now often referred to as axiomatically true, whereas it is an inference, the evidence for which, even to many realists, is far from conclusive. Whether it be considered true or not in science, physical evolution is quite untrue in philosophy.

IDEAS

VIII—HOW PRODUCED

An imprint or mould of the object is generally left in the plasma of the subject. The imprint is deep, clear and lasting in proportion to the strength of the exciting cause and the degree of energy assigned to the perception. When the noumenon withdraws the object does not at once disappear, for if the energy of attention remain the mould left by the noumenon serves to excite a consciousness similar to the object, and this is what we call an IDEA.

What Hume says as to an object differing from an idea in nothing but vividness is evidently incorrect. Objects are generally, but not always, more vivid than ideas, and when an object is present we have an indefeasible conviction of being acted on by something not ourselves, which conviction is not present in recollection. We may not be able to give a satisfactory reason for the conviction—if we are arguing idealistically we certainly shall not—but the fact that it is there serves to mark off objects as a class of consciousness distinct from ideas, irrespective of their vividness. If an object were once seen clearly and so remembered, and were afterwards seen indistinctly through a mist, the latter consciousness would (according to Hume) be the idea and the former the object. Such an application of words would be an abuse of language.

There are of course no innate ideas of *objects*. There is innate consciousness—the sentimental.

Ideas are of three kinds—Particular Ideas, General Ideas, Imaginary Ideas—corresponding to the so-called faculties of Memory, Generalisation or Classification, and Imagination.

IX—MEMORY OF OBJECTS

When the energy of attention is exhausted or withdrawn the idea also disappears, but it may be revived by bringing the energised Self in contact with the imprint again, and this operation can be repeated indefinitely. The power of exciting ideas of past experience is Memory; any particular exercise of memory is Recollection.

The imprint of an object is not absolutely permanent and is probably never quite true. It begins to lose sharpness at once, but if the object be frequently observed and much remembered, it will retain its general character for years. The exercise of memory, instead of wearing out the imprint as would be the case with a material negative or engraved plate, keeps the channels open[1]. Persons of little experience remember well, for their energy of attention is not distributed over many different ideas; it travels continuously round a small circuit. One hears ignorant persons recounting events that happened years ago, with as much detail and with almost as much sentiment as if they had taken place the day before. A 'good memory' is no proof that the quality of mind or thought is good. All experience is not worth remembering. One of the most difficult things in moral culture is to get rid of the imprints of ideas that are out of harmony with our improved sentiment.

Although the imprints in our mind may close up and leave scarce a cicatrice, the part that has been once disturbed is never the same as the virgin plasm. It remains a little more tender. It may not reopen to ordinary stimuli, but an extra agitation of the plasm

[1] As if the image had the form of a stencil.

will rip up the closed furrows, and give us back scenes in our life that had long ceased to be recollected. A great agitation in all parts of the mind may revive what appears to be the whole of our past experience in a simultaneous recollection. So I explain the extraordinary lucidity that sometimes occurs in fevers and in moments of extreme terror.

It is also conceivable that the egoistic energy may be so strong as to destroy outright the moulds of thought, as a flood sweeps away the banks of a river. 'We sometimes find a disease quite strip the mind of all its ideas, and the flames of a fever in a few days calcine all those images to dust and confusion which seemed to be as lasting as if graved in marble'[1].

What is called 'decay of the mind' in old age is merely the loss of the plasmic images. Since intellect would not have been formed in the first instance if it had not been wanted, it is to be expected that it will fade out of the mind when it is no longer wanted. So far as the realistic intellect is concerned, we return to 'second childhood' and the uniform sensibility we had at birth.

No philosophy but the substantial explains memory. Idealists and metaphysicians, who recognise only consciousness, are utterly unable to account for

---

[1] Locke, *Essay on the Understanding*, ii. x. 5.

the revival of a shadowy sort of objects in the absence of their original causes. Here is the melancholy confession of John Stuart Mill on the subject:—

'If we speak of the Mind as a series of feelings, we are obliged to complete the statement by calling it a series of feelings which is aware of itself as past and future: and we are reduced to the alternative of believing that the Mind, or Ego, is something different from any series of feelings, or possibilities of them, or of accepting the paradox that something which *ex hypothesi* is but a series of feelings, can be aware of itself as a series.

'The truth is that we are here face to face with that final inexplicability at which, as Sir W. Hamilton observes, we inevitably arrive when we reach ultimate facts; and in general one mode of stating it only appears more incomprehensible than another, because the whole of human language is accommodated to the one, and is so incongruous with the other, that it cannot be expressed in any terms which do not deny its truth. The real stumbling-block is perhaps not in any theory of the fact, but in the fact itself. The true incomprehensibility perhaps is, that something which has ceased, or is not yet in existence, can still be, in a manner, present: that a series of feelings, the infinitely greater part of which is past or future, can be gathered up as it were into a single present conception, accompanied by a belief of reality. I think, by far the wisest thing we can do is to accept the inexplicable fact, without any theory of how it takes place; and when we are obliged to speak of it in terms which assume a theory, to use them with a reservation as to their meaning¹.'

Memory an ultimate fact! It is the first that stares us in the face on beginning to philosophise, and it haunts us through all our subsequent speculations. It is the 'dweller on the threshold' of philosophy, which unless we overcome will overcome us, and frustrate our magic.

The passage quoted does not show Mill's usual candour and consistency. His philosophy has broken down on an essential point, and he is reluctant to admit it. He tries to throw the blame on other things, and recommends that those who think with him should maintain a discreet silence on the subject of memory, or if obliged to speak of it do so in ambiguous language. That is hardly honest, and is bad philosophical practice. What we know or think we know we may leave alone—it will not run away; it is what we are conscious of not knowing that should receive our persistent attention.

Materialism presents at first sight the data out of which to construct a theory of memory, for it recognises the dependent character of consciousness and takes body to be its substance. Does the body show any marks or traces of thought that may serve to

[1] *Exam. of Hamilton's Philosophy*, p. 212-3.

revive ideas in the absence of objects? None have yet been discovered. Nerves are used in objective observation, but they do not appear to be essential either to recollection in general or to any of the more elaborate forms of internal thought. The brain is used only when giving expression to thought.

Memory is noticed by everyone, even the least metaphysical. Persons who are incapable of understanding the difference between object and subject or general and particular, are yet perfectly well aware of the difference between remembering and forgetting. The phrases relating to this distinction are the commonest in every language. Memory is conspicuous—notorious—palpable. It is the pivot on which the whole mental system revolves. It cannot be gainsaid or ignored. There is no profit in boycotting it in the manner recommended by Mill—it must be faced and explained. 'How do you account for memory?' should be the first question addressed to one who pretends to have a science of mind. If he has no plausible answer to give, his system is not worth discussion. A philosophy without a theory of memory is like an astronomy without gravitation.

X — MEMORY OF SENTIMENTS

SENTIMENTS are remembered and recollected like objects. For instance, a boy is punished for doing wrong and has *pain*; he does wrong again and is haunted with the *fear* of being punished again, which is the recollected and anticipated pain. We have thus two species of sentiment corresponding exactly to object and idea. The word 'feeling' is appropriate to the first, 'emotion' to the second. 'Passion' is a strong degree of either.

Objects that are associated with feelings are better remembered than those that merely affect the intellect, for there is a double memory at work—one in the core and one on the surface of our mind.

Sentiments are not susceptible of the same degree of analysis as objects. The inner matrix is more fluid and does not keep details. Apart from the objects associated with feelings, there is not much opportunity or need for classifying them. We are happy, wretched, or indifferent—that sums up the sentimental experience.

No two moral philosophers give the same list of sentiments. Some are satisfied with two—pain and pleasure. Spinoza gives a list of forty-seven [1] sentiments, which includes luxury and drunkenness. It is evident that luxury is a general term which covers many different forms of feeling, and if the feeling of intoxication by alcohol is worth mentioning, so also must be the intoxications by opium and tobacco; and if these are included we must admit the feeling of nausea, which brings us to the sentiments associated with all diseased conditions of body or mind. Such distinctions are superfluous, for if the sentiment is purely personal and not associated with an external object, it is not of any general interest; if associated with an object and common to many persons it is best defined by reference to the object—as the pleasure of smelling a *rose*.

We have sometimes feelings of elation and depression for which we cannot find an internal reason nor yet an objective sign. Many of the so-called religious experiences are of this sort. So also are the sudden sympathies and aversions we feel towards certain people and places. Here there is an object, but we

[1] I append Spinoza's list, and print in italics the sentiments that appear to me to be emotions as distinguished from feelings. Desire — Pleasure — Pain — Wonder — *Contempt* — *Love* — *Hate* — *Inclination*—*Aversion*— Devotion— Derision— *Hope*—*Fear*—*Confidence*—*Despair*—Joy— Grief—Pity—Approval—Indignation—Overesteem— *Disparagement*—*Envy*—Mercy(or goodwill)—Self-contentment—Humility —*Repentance*—*Pride*—Dejection— Honour— *Shame*—*Regret*—*Emulation*— Thankfulness— Benevolence— Anger—*Revenge*—Cruelty—*Daring*—*Cowardice*—*Consternation*—*Civility* (or deference)—*Ambition*— Luxury—Drunkenness—Avarice—Lust. Pollock's *Spinoza*, ch. vii.

cannot find anything in the object that can be taken as specially significant of the feeling. We are said not to be able to 'analyse' our feeling, that is, assign it an object as cause.

These abnormal feelings may be explained by supposing that some external influences succeed in reaching our sentiment without exciting our intellect. Considering that intellect is artificial and may be very imperfect, and also that its efficiency depends to some extent on its being less sensitive than the original mental nature, it is reasonable to conclude that subtle emanations from our surroundings may occasionally affect us without exciting the intellectual consciousness. Panic, inspiration, mesmerism, and other 'occult' influences are probably due to this cause. If we further assume that sentiments so excited may then, by association, excite appropriate *ideas* in the intellect of the recipient, we have a likely explanation of what is called 'thought-transference.' Since ideas excite emotions, it is reasonable to suppose that feelings may excite ideas, or even the illusion that objects are being perceived.

XI—COMPARISON

MOST ideas, except the particular (which are copies

of single objects), are associated with a consciousness of resemblance and difference which arises in the following manner.

When new experience simply revives the imprint of a former experience we call it the *same* object or objects, though it is not numerically the same, being different at least in time. If a totally new imprint is made in the mind the experience is quite novel or *strange*, but we do not call it different.

Experience is usually neither quite the same as before nor quite strange, which means that the present noumenon has partially revived an old imprint and made a partially new one.

In this case we have a quadruple consciousness. There is first the present object; next the recollection of the object originally associated with the same imprint; thirdly, a consciousness of *resemblance* between the new and the old (the present object and the recollected idea) in so far as the imprints coincide, and (fourthly) a sense of *difference* in so far as they disagree. The limitation of resemblance gives rise to the sense of difference—a negative consciousness—and the shock of difference emphasises the resemblance. This is Comparison, the common basis of Generalisation and Imagination.

GENERALISATION

XII—NATURE AND FUNCTION

GENERAL IDEAS are formed by the coincident imprint of several objects in some respects different, but which have all a resemblance as objects, and are besides the signs of the same sentimental effect. If the effects are different the confusion of the objects occasions practical error, as when we mistake one man for another whom he closely resembles. Though the sentimental utilities should be the same, the object cannot be reduced to a common idea if they are quite dissimilar: for example, a sand-glass and a watch have similar uses, but they cannot be generalized. The value of generalisation to a thinker is that it economises memory and recollection by making one common or average idea do duty for many particular ideas. Let us follow the process in detail.

The first perception of an object leaves an imprint in the substance of the intellect. A second perception partially resembling the first revives the first to the extent at least of the resemblance. Supposing this is done by a hundred similar objects it is plain that the resembling properties will have been experienced a hundred times, whereas the distinguishing attributes may have been felt a few times only, in some cases only once. Unless we have special reasons for observing the differences and so deepening the impressions of them, they will fade from our memory at a rate corresponding to the paucity of experiences. The most general idea will last longest because *there* the impression has been very deep. Our idea of Man or Animal will on this principle, as it is found to do in fact, outlast our memory of many concrete men and animals.

The objects that contribute to form a general idea or Class are commonly said to 'belong to,' or to 'inhere in,' or to be 'brought under' the idea or class. All these metaphors are wrong and occasion mistakes. Generalisation is nothing but condensed or epitomised recollection; it is practised by ourselves for our own convenience, and does not imply any essential or extra-personal relation between the objects. We are free to classify things in any order we find useful.

A farmer's classification of some animals into cattle, game, fowls, birds, and vermin, is perfectly legitimate, for each species is based on a different utility for him.

We should distinguish general ideas which we ourselves have drawn from our primary experience, from the ideas suggested by verbal definitions of general ideas formed by other minds. Supposing the objects in question to be quite unknown to us, the definitional idea is more like a particular or imaginary idea than a general idea. It is a single thin rigid idea, utterly unlike the flexible suggestive thought evolved from a large mass of personal experience. Definitional general ideas are as unsatisfactory as described objects, but we are sometimes compelled to use both when personal experience is totally wanting.

It is a common error to suppose that general ideas cannot exist in the intellect without words by which to name them. Words and other modes of marking ideas are useful in all departments of thought, but not more necessary in general thought than in any other. An active intellect makes thousands of observations and scores of general ideas which it may have no means or wish to express in language.

Generalisation is very like the operation called composite photography. A number of persons are posed in the same attitude and partially photographed on the same plate. The result is an average or mean likeness of the whole group, but not an exact portrait of any individual. So general ideas are 'means' or 'averages' of many resembling but slightly differing objects.

There are other things in the photographic art remarkably similar to intellectual thinking. The gelatine film behaves very like the mental plasma: only one other physical object (so far as I am aware) is a better image of the plasm.

In theory the object or phenomenon has no importance. Even when it has the quality we call 'beauty,' that is not a property of the bare object, for it is not seen by every person or animal with good eyesight; it is a sentimental effect associated with the object. Hence we might, if it were possible, ignore all objects except those which have value to us as signs of sentimental effects.

But in practice we cannot do this. Objects are thrust upon our notice which we cannot avoid, and which have no sentimental interest for us. These objects are necessarily classified according to their phenomenal appearance only, and such ideas lack an essential characteristic of true general ideas. But we cannot prevent their formation in the mind, for generalisation is merely a kind of abbreviated memory, and, objects being once perceived, their recollection is to a great extent beyond our control.

Artificial and adventitious utilities produce the same kind of one-sided generalisation. If society pays a man in fame or money to observe and describe certain things, his classification of them will be purely phenomenal. He will classify dogs with wolves and nightshade with potato, and will lump together the whole population of a country in one class, although it consists of the most divers elements—fools and philosophers, rogues and righteous, saints and sinners, patricians and plebeians. These are differences much more important than sameness of nationality, colour, race, or language.

This practice, no doubt, gives symmetrical classifications. The greater classes are subdivided into subordinate classes, and these again into lower classes in a many-stepped series. Gradation occurs also in true generalisation, but not to the same extent.

If we confine our observation to things that are much like each other, the average idea will not be greatly different from a particular idea: this is called *lowness* in generality. If we run together quadrupeds, bipeds and fishes, we shall have a much higher general idea: the average will be very unlike any concrete animal. The higher we generalise the smaller becomes the content of the idea, but the wider its extension, that is, the realm of objects from which it has been drawn, or which it is considered to represent. The usual practice is to generalise by fine gradations. Get the general idea of sheep, then of cow, then of horse; then average the averages. The result is much the same if we run all the objects together and average them in one operation, but the slower process gives the neater results. The gradations of generality are distinguished by names such as (beginning from below) variety, species, genus, class, family, kingdom.

'Conceptualism' is the metaphysical doctrine now prevalent with respect to general ideas. They are regarded not as objects nor as essences, but as forms of consciousness depending more or less on our own mental activity. This is true enough so far as it goes, but without a substantial plasm to hold the 'concept' its formation and endurance are quite inexplicable.

XIII—MATTER

MATTER is the name given to the most general idea we can form of objects. It is supposed to cover all of them. In other words, the content or 'essence' of the idea is the attribute or attributes common to all objects without exception. It is the universal objective minimum—the least objective experience consistent with the experience being objective. Some have attempted to define this general idea more precisely by identifying it with some *abstract* property such as extension, resistance, etc. An object may be material without offering any resistance to human energy, as a beam of light. A material object may also be without extension, as a sound or smell. The only quality left to matter is bare objectivity, namely, that it is a form of consciousness excited in a mind by some other mind, not occurring spontaneously. This seems to me the only true connotation of matter.

Matter is not the antithesis of mind; it is a mere affection of mind. The two are not in any proper sense co-ordinate or equipollent. They are to each other somewhat in the relation of a mirror to an image reflected from it. Mind is to each of us a concrete primary experience—the feeling of personal power and identity. Matter is a general idea arising from the comparison of objects in consciousness. No two things could well be more diverse.

Since general ideas are products of our own mental energy, and matter the most general of all, it is the farthest removed from the concrete objective condition, and so it is literally true that we never objectively perceive matter though we constantly perceive material objects. It is as impossible to see, touch, or taste matter as it is to ride the general idea *Equus* or dine off the general idea *nourishment*. In denying the objectivity of matter we do not deny the objective reality of things: we merely decline to confound a general idea with the objects that have contributed to form it. We decline to be *mystics*, in the sense defined by J. S. Mill[1]. The belief in the external existence of matter is a form of mysticism; the Hindus call it *maya*, meaning illusion.

Some metaphysicians argue that since phenomena appear only in conjunction, we are compelled by the constitution of our nature to think of them conjoined in and by something, and this imaginary foundation and cement is another meaning of the word 'matter.'

For myself I feel no such compulsion. When things are complex I recollect the several properties as cohering together, and when I abstract one or some for special consideration, I sometimes think of the others as forming a 'substance' in which the abstracted properties inhere. But I cannot discover any inherence or coherence except the mutual, and the notion of an invisible material setting which holds all the parts of a thing together seems to me superfluous and unwarranted. If it existed it would not be, as logicians argue, something superior and antithetical

---

[1] 'Mysticism is neither more nor less than ascribing objective existence to the subjective creations of our own faculties, to ideas or feelings of the mind.'—*Logic*, chapter on 'Fallacies.'

to phenomena; it would be simply an inferred or latent phenomenon like the luminiferous ether of science. The material substance is evidently a groping of the mind after the noumenal (mental) substance which causes the appearance of objects.

XIV—NOMINALISM

NOMINALISTS deny the existence of general ideas as distinct from particular ideas. Most of them affirm that we employ general or common words to signify the common properties of similar things, but that we are incapable of thinking of these common properties apart from the other properties that accompany them.

Why we should wish to use signs of things we cannot think about, or how a word can be a 'sign' when we are incapable of attaching a definite meaning to it, are points not satisfactorily cleared up by nominalists.

Considering how well Berkeley's principle, combined with the plasmic theory, accounts for generalisation, and how inevitable it is that there should be general ideas distinguishable from particular ideas by superior brilliancy and endurance, it is surprising to find in Berkeley one of the most convinced and eloquent of **nominalists**. His views on the subject have so much weight with philosophers that I must examine them at length.

'It is agreed on all hands,' he writes in the Introduction to his *Principles*, 'that the qualities or modes of things do never really exist each of them apart by itself, and separated from all others, but are mixed, as it were, and blended together, several in the same object. But, we are told, the mind being able to consider each quality singly, or abstracted from those other qualities with which it is united, does by that means frame to itself abstract ideas. For example, there is perceived by sight an object extended, coloured, and moved: this mixed or compound idea the mind resolving into its simple constituent parts, and viewing each by itself, exclusive of the rest, does frame the abstract ideas of extension, colour, and motion. Not that it is possible for colour or motion to exist without extension; but only that the mind can frame to itself by *abstraction* the idea of colour exclusive of extension, and of motion exclusive of both colour and extension.'

Abstract ideas do not form a fourth class of ideas but are fractions of particular, general, or imaginary ideas, and may (as Berkeley, reporting the metaphysical doctrine, says) be single or partial properties mentally detached from the collective properties forming an object. In this case they are abstracted properties, not ideas. Since general ideas are less complete than the particular ideas from which they were drawn, they are abstract ideas in so far as they are partial ideas; but all abstract ideas are not general ideas. Berkeley's nominalism is based on the supposed impossibility of forming any sort of partial idea, and he now proceeds to reproduce the metaphysical account of the general abstract idea.

'And as the mind frames to itself abstract ideas of qualities or modes, so does it, by the same precision or mental separation, attain abstract ideas [general ideas] of the more compounded beings which include several co-existent qualities. For example, the mind having observed that Peter, James, and John resemble each other in certain common agreements of shape and other qualities, leaves out of the complex or compounded idea it has of Peter, James, and any other particular man, that which is peculiar to each, retaining only what is common to all, and so makes an abstract [general] idea wherein all the particulars equally partake—abstracting entirely from and cutting off those circumstances and differences which might determine it to any particular existence. And after this manner it is said we come by the abstract [general] idea of man, or, if you please, humanity or human nature; wherein it is true there is included colour, because there is no man but has some colour, but then it can be neither white, nor black, nor any particular colour, because there is no one particular colour wherein all men partake. So likewise there is included stature, but then it is neither tall stature, nor low stature, nor yet middle stature, but something abstracted from all these. And so of the rest. Moreover, there being a great variety of other creatures that partake of some parts, but not all, of the complex idea of man, the mind, leaving out those parts which are peculiar to men, and retaining those only which are common to all the living creatures, frames the idea of *animal*, which abstracts not only from all particular men, but also all birds, beasts, fishes and insects. The constituent parts of the abstract idea of animal are body, life, sense, and spontaneous motion. By *body* is meant body without any particular shape or figure, there being no one shape or figure common to all animals, without covering either of hair, or feathers, or scales, &c., nor yet naked: hair, feathers, scales, and nakedness being the distinguishing properties of particular animals, and for that reason left out of the *abstract* [general] *idea*. Upon the same account the spontaneous motion must be neither walking, nor flying, nor creeping; it is nevertheless a motion, but what that motion is it is not easy to conceive.'

This is a fair paraphrase of the accounts given by metaphysicians of the manner of forming general ideas. It is also in itself a perfectly correct account of the process, considered simply as a manifestation of consciousness or a succession of states of consciousness, that is, apart from the substantial plasmic operation of which it is merely the symptom. Berkeley however denies that it is a true statement of what takes place in the mind of consciousness.

'Whether others have this wonderful faculty of abstracting their ideas, they best can tell; for myself, I find indeed I have a faculty of imagining or representing to myself, the ideas of those particular things I have perceived, and of variously compounding and dividing them. I can imagine a man with two heads, or the upper parts of a man joined to the body of a horse. I can consider the hand, the eye, the nose each by itself abstracted or separated from the rest of the body. But then, whatever hand or eye I imagine, it must have some particular shape or colour. Likewise the idea of man that I frame to myself must be either of a white, or a black, or a tawny, a straight, or a crooked, a tall, or a low, or a middle-sized man. I cannot by any effort of thought conceive the abstract idea above described. And it is equally impossible for me to form the abstract idea of motion distinct from the body moving, and which is neither swift nor slow, curvilinear nor rectilinear; and the like may be said of all other abstract general ideas whatsoever. To be plain, I own myself able to abstract in one sense, as when I consider some particular parts or qualities separated from others, and which, though they are united in some object, yet it is possible they may really exist without them. But I deny that I can abstract from one another, or conceive separately, those qualities which it is impossible should exist so separated; or that I can form a general notion, by abstracting from particulars in the manner aforesaid—which last are the two proper acceptations of *abstraction*. And there is ground to think most men will acknowledge themselves to be in my case. The generality of men which are simple and illiterate never pretend to *abstract notions* [general ideas]. It is said they are difficult and not to be attained without pains and study; we may therefore reasonably conclude that, if such there be, they are confined only to the learned.'

It is quite true that 'the simple and illiterate never *pretend* to abstract notions,' for the sufficient reason that they do not know the names of their mental operations, even if they are capable of discriminating them. For the same reason they do not pretend to talk prose or to be realists.

The practice of every profession and craft, even the humblest, involves abstraction and generalisation. The objective properties associated with a given utility have to be abstracted from those which are indifferent, and this is what enables men of experience in any branch of industry or art to form a speedy judgment on matters touching their special affairs. It is in part what distinguishes the 'professional' from the 'amateur.'

Berkeley's disclaimer of any power in himself to form general ideas is no doubt sincere, and he is justified in reasoning from himself to others. But the point at issue is, whether Berkeley in this instance correctly analysed his own mental processes. The fact that he was correct in some points of great importance does not preclude us from surmising that he may have been wrong in others of less importance. In comparison with his discovery of the substantiality of mind, his oversight on the subject of abstraction is a bagatelle.

He explains the existence of general words on the theory that they are names of particular ideas which we use to represent all similar ideas.

'... an idea which, considered in itself, is particular, becomes general by being made to represent or stand for all other particular ideas of the same sort. To make this plain by an example, suppose a geometrician is demonstrating the method of cutting a line in two equal parts. He draws, for instance, a black line of one inch in length: this, which in itself is a particular line, is nevertheless with regard to its signification general, since, as it is there used, it represents all particular lines whatsoever; so that what is demonstrated of it is demonstrated of all lines, or, in other words, of a line in general. And, as *that particular line* becomes general by being made a sign, so the *name* " line," which taken absolutely is particular, by being a sign is made general. And as the former owes its generality not to its being the sign of an abstract or general line, but of all particular right lines that may possibly exist, so the latter must be thought to derive its generality from the same cause, namely, the various particular lines which it indifferently denotes.'

Nominalism

These extracts will suffice to show what was Berkeley's doctrine on the subject of general ideas.

With respect to the analogy supposed to exist between the generality of a name and the generality of a general idea, it has to be observed that a name owes its generality solely to its being the sign of a general idea. It is an imputed or conventional generality,—in its proper character a general name is concrete and individual. Also it does not resemble the thing it signifies (the general idea), nor the concrete things from which that has been derived.

The generality of a general idea, on the other hand, depends altogether on its *resemblance* to many particular things. It is independent of convention. Hence there is no real analogy between the two generalities.

Considering that Berkeley professes himself unable to imagine abstract properties, it is surprising how easily and naturally he writes about geometrical lines —which are abstract properties. Probably he means concrete *strokes*.

What sort of representation can subsist between one concrete stroke and every other concrete stroke? If it is straight it will not correctly represent a curve; if it is curved it will not represent a straight stroke. A stroke an inch long cannot stand for a stroke a hundred miles long; a black stroke does not properly represent a red stroke. So it is incorrect to say that 'what is demonstrated of *it* is demonstrated of all strokes, or, in other words, of a stroke in general.' A particular object can stand only for itself, and if general words stand for many things it is not by direct representation, but because they first suggest general ideas, which are the true substitutes of many particular things.

A reference to geometrical objects, themselves so abstract, is a doubtful mode of showing how well one concrete thing can represent others. Had Berkeley taken a more complex object as his general representative he would have seen the weakness of his argument. Suppose a biologist has to discourse on a province of animal life comprising many species, and takes an individual of one species as a representative of the whole. His sample is perhaps a hare, but he has to treat of birds and fishes. What is to prevent his hearers from concluding that birds are furred animals and fishes quadrupeds? Are they to be expected to see in the hare only the properties common to all the animals reviewed? If so they have the power denied them by nominalists of forming a pure general idea, and the hare is superfluous. The common properties could have been defined and imagined without a concrete specimen, with irrelevant attributes, being brought into the discourse.

All nominalists insist that if we think long on a

general idea it becomes particular, and from this they argue that it is not, and never has been, a general idea [1].

The experiments of this sort proposed by logicians are misleading, because we are without the ordinary motives for thinking generally. In practical thought we have some sufficient reason for attending to a fraction of consciousness and excluding the rest, and the irrelevant qualities are distinctly less charged with attention than the principal quality.

The power of abstracting thought is a matter of education. It is that ruling of the spirit which is more difficult than the capture of a city. We have to master the restless energic Self and fix it down on a particular plasmic figure, or a mere point or edge of one, preventing the energy from spreading to adjacent images. That is irksome and fatiguing, but it is only a high degree of the faculty everyone possesses of distinguishing particular objects from each other. Some minds are so flaccid that you cannot hold them to one subject, even the most particular and obvious, for five minutes at a time. Training enables us to bring into the focus of attention just what we wish to observe or think about, and

---

[1] With equal plausibility it might be argued that we have no particular ideas, because it is difficult if not impossible to observe and remember all the details of any object. Our most particular ideas are slightly abstract, and in the process of forgetting they become more and more abstract, until they disappear altogether.

leave the rest in the background, however closely it may be connected with the matter that immediately interests us. But for this power much of our energy would be expended to no purpose. Abstraction is simply attention of a minute and concentrated kind —a bringing of our energy of observation or recollection to a fine point.

When abstraction need not be prolonged—when we are free to pass rapidly from one general or abstract idea to another—there is no difficulty in partial thinking. We skim over the plasmic imprints, lightly brushing the surface of each where it is most prominent and therefore most general, but not pausing to recollect particulars. It is this rapid delicate touch we oftenest use in actual thought; but when for purposes of experiment we come down heavily on an imprint, then the Self overflows to adjacent channels and particular memories are stirred up, in spite of every effort to limit our attention.

So common and easy is rapid general thought that it is constantly used as a substitute for concrete thought, when a sketchy treatment of things is all that is wanted.

'A bird has alighted on the fence.' The speaker saw a particular concrete bird, and might have tried to describe it in the concrete. But the attributes that rendered it concrete are supposed not to be of present importance, and the hearer is consequently invited to think only of bird in general. Would a nominalist affirm that in such a case the words are meaningless unless the idea is concreted—unless the general sketch is filled out in detail?

Take another example. 'The man sat by the window overlooking the river that flowed towards the city.'

Here all the nouns are general, but the picture is individual and concrete. It is also quite intelligible, as a sketch. We can think of a man without assigning to him any particular type of face, or colour of hair, or stature, or age, or clothing. Our idea is the general idea *man* used as a sketch of a particular man. He is in a house because he is looking through a window, but we do not stay to imagine the house as cottage, inn, or mansion. We call up the general idea *house*, which is definite enough for our purpose, and we cannot doubt for a moment that we have such a general idea. The river may be wide or narrow, straight or crooked, navigable or not, but we think only of the general idea *river*, which is water flowing between banks. And surely we can imagine a general *city* without giving it any definite size, or form, or nationality, or number of inhabitants!

These considerations clearly demonstrate that we have general ideas, which are not merely concrete ideas used as examples, and if we can employ them in the manner just indicated, where a light superficial recollection is all that is necessary, we can equally well use them in their more legitimate character, as signs of certain general utilities.

XV—ERRORS WITH RESPECT TO GENERALISATION

GENERALISATION has been the bane of European philosophy. It has monopolised well-nigh the whole metaphysical attention. It has been considered the radical fact of mind from which all others have grown, whereas it is no more than a method for abbreviating recollection. It neither reveals to us new things, nor reduces the multiplicity of things actually existing.

Plato insisted on the importance of general thought as against the fluctional idealism of Heraclitus, but he was wholly mistaken as to the nature of general ideas. He thought they were external objects—also types and causes of primary objects. But patterns are not causes, and general ideas are quite obviously suggested by things, not things derived from general ideas. The notion that the general idea is either the cause, or an image and revelation of the cause, of things is an error of perennial recurrence. In some form or other it is always with us.

Plato also taught that general ideas are recollections of knowledge acquired in the condition prior to embodiment, which the objective experience of this life serves to revive. These several doctrines are somewhat inconsistent with each other. The last is interesting but lacks confirmation.

Aristotle admitted the superiority of general over particular ideas, and thought that the former corresponded to some specially important part of objects called the 'essence.'

This is nearer the truth. The essence of an object is that part of it, which being present, a given sentimental result follows, or may be expected to follow, or may be made to follow. A certain experience of things is necessary before we can know what is the objective minimum consistent with some sentimental utility. If things are classified with due regard to their utilities, the essence will be the same as the general idea. It is however not true that the essence or any other part of the object causes the sentimental effect (VII).

A common form of the generalistic superstition is to suppose that a thing is explained or sufficiently accounted for by classifying it.

In all philosophies of Greek derivation—the Asiatic

seem to be free from this defect—reason is considered to be 'the bringing of a thing under a class-notion,' and when this is done we are supposed to know the thing completely. An elaborate and utterly false dialectic has been erected on this foundation.

No doubt our first attempt at explaining a thing is to refer it to a general idea—to classify it. This usually suggests something to add to the bare phenomenon by way of explanation or hypothesis. But only if we have a prior knowledge of the general idea, derived from things better known than the present phenomenon. The general idea is simply a short formula of that prior knowledge. Suppose we thoroughly know a body of similar things a, b, c, and also reduce them to the general image X; then on seeing d and noticing that it is like a, b, c, we briefly think, 'Oh, it is X,' which excuses us from studying it further. We at once transfer to d our whole knowledge of a, b, c, and in this ideal transfer the explanation consists—not in the classification. The transfer is often tacit—if explicit it is an 'argument.'

If there has been no better known a, b, c, it is evident that the mere generalisation of new facts d, e, f, will not add anything to our knowledge of them. In deduction we should only return to them the knowledge just extracted from them. We should be explaining things by themselves—reasoning in a circle¹.

The *unity* which explains is not the general idea. It is a unity of function or service, and may include things utterly heterogeneous, and therefore incapable of being reduced to a common idea. The pen in my hand consists of wood and metal; if I generalise them into Matter—the nearest class that includes both—I do not thereby explain the pen. But it is explained by the unity of service: the wood and metal contribute to form one instrument for writing.

The best results of modern science are discoveries of utilities (inventions); discoveries of the relations of sequence among objects, which enable us to predict their arrival years in advance; of coexistences on the great cosmic scale (geographical and stellar exploration); of co-inherence of properties in individual objects (chemistry). Yet science is still too generalistic. It runs too much to classification and nomenclature, which is nothing but *memoria technica*.

---

¹ Mill's nominalistic tendencies led him to the same conclusion: 'Our general ideas contain nothing but what has been put into them, either by our passive experience, or by our active habits of thought; and the metaphysicians in all ages, who have attempted to construct the laws of the universe by reasoning from our supposed necessities of thought, have always proceeded, and only could proceed, by laboriously finding in their own minds what they themselves had formerly put there, and evolving from their ideas of things what they had first involved in those ideas.'—*Logic*, Bk. V. c. 3. § 3.

Modern biology presents a curious return of Platonism. The general idea is not indeed put forward as the cause of individuals, but a particular concrete animal is found who closely resembles the general idea, and it is imagined that an animal like him was the original cause of all animals of his species. When it happens—as it occasionally must in a thorough-going system of phenomenal classification—that the average or general idea falls between two species, no individual can be found to represent it with the desired exactness. In this case it is supposed by evolutionists that the intermediate animal has existed but is now extinct. These are the 'missing links' so badly wanted to complete the evolutionary scheme.

IMAGINATION

XVI

This faculty or habit consists essentially in combining ideas (particular or general), or objects and ideas, so as to form systems different from those occurring in actual experience. The whole has never been perceived, though all its elements have been perceived.

Any association of ideas may be called imaginary if it occurs in an order different from the order of experience. But the term Imagination is properly confined to novel combinations deliberately and consciously formed to serve some utility. It is thus distinguished from Reverie, in which no choice or control enters into the recollection.

We control our ideal associations by means of comparison, which is therefore what distinguishes imagination from reverie. For instance, if I see a vase from which the handle has been broken off, I can imagine the handle restored, but to do this I must be able to compare the broken vase with a similar whole vase, or with the general idea 'whole vase.' The combination I form is novel, for I have never seen this particular vase in a whole state; if I had I should not be imagining it but recollecting it.

There are two principal distinctions to be noticed in imagination; one relates to the mode of forming the imaginary idea, the other to its use.

In the above case we form the whole by mechanical extension or addition. The process is as simple as nailing one piece of wood to another. But suppose the broken vase is of porcelain and the whole one of bronze, the restoration can still be made, but it is no mechanical junction of two previous ideas. It is a fusion of the material supplied by one idea with a form supplied by another. On the same principle a vase may be wholly designed from hints supplied by a score or more of vases, differing in material, in size, colour, decoration, and so forth. In these cases the new idea may be said to be totally different throughout its length from any other and from any object. Yet it is a combination of previous ideas. We do not create any absolutely new idea. This may be called imagination by *transfusion*. The elements may be so well mixed that it is impossible to trace each back to its origin.

Transfusion may be further complicated by re-compounding ideas already compound. This occurs, as we shall see, in forming the 'external world' of materialists and realists.

The two uses to which imaginary ideas are put are the Artistic and the Rational.

We have seen (x) that emotions may be excited by objects or ideas. Hence, agreeable emotions may be excited by suggesting the objects associated with the original agreeable feelings; and novel emotions may be excited by novel combinations of the ideas of experienced objects that have been signs of feelings. From this possibility has arisen that extensive province of activity called ART, which consists in imagining novel combinations of things capable of exciting novel and pleasurable emotions (not feelings), and in finding means of suggesting such ideas to others. Some of these combinations are so subtle, and the emotions they excite so exquisite, that we value the artistic work at a great price, and rank the man who imagined it among the benefactors of his species.

REASON, or the Rational Imagination, does not appeal directly to the emotions. It serves the uses of life by enabling us to imagine what we have not yet experienced but may have to experience, and the quality aimed at is accuracy of intellectual ideation, not emotional pleasure. It is found by experience that an intellect well furnished with ideas may learn to combine them into pictures or preconceptions of the future, and the indirect utility of this accomplishment is very great. If it does not, like art, give immediate sentimental pleasure, it often enables us so to control events that we are brought into conditions affording more lasting satisfaction than many expensive works of art. Reason, then, is the imaginative faculty applied to the purpose of acquiring ideas of experience that has not yet taken place, and it is good in proportion to the similarity of the idea to the anticipated or unknown experience.

Although imagination is more important than generalisation, it has received little attention from metaphysicians. Their treatment of it is not uniform, but it generally exhibits two fundamental defects. They consider it an independent or ultimate faculty, that is, one incapable of resolution into anything more simple. We have seen that it is an application of comparison, and comparison depends on the coincidence of particular ideas.

Then they regard imagination only in its artistic uses, not perceiving that it is also the basis of reason. Reason they treat as generalisation—a vice that pervades all their systems. They put reason and art in essential opposition, whereas the difference between them is only specific—a difference of use.

Some metaphysicians confound imagination with mere recollection. 'It is,' says one of them, 'the faculty representative of the phenomena both of the external and internal worlds.' But there is a great difference between the representation of what we have experienced actually, and the representation of a future and perhaps impossible event: the latter only is imaginative. 'There is no train of ideas,' says another, 'to which the term imagination may not be applied.' If a man at the end of the day calls to mind all the events of the day in a train of ideas, that is recollection, and would be very inappropriately termed imagination. According to a third, imagination has for its object the concrete as opposed to abstractions and generalities. This also is inexact. A traveller may describe in general the qualities of a foreign country or tribe of men, and we shall imagine that generality without a concrete picture. The power of imagining generalities and abstractions necessarily follows from the power of forming them in the first instance.

DIALECTIC

XVII—ITS SCOPE

THE derivation of Reason as given in the preceding sections may be summed up thus:—the meeting of Minds gives Perception or primary experience; Attention selects therefrom objects of special interest to the observer; Memory retains impressions of these in the mental plasma, by which ideas of them are recollected though the originating mind be not present; community with divergence of imprint gives rise to Comparison; from this are derived Imagination and Generalisation; from imagination emerge Reason and Art.

Generalisation is thus only a collateral relation of reason, not its immediate parent nor in the direct line of descent. It is not essential to reason, but may enter as a subsidiary process into an argument. If the things we argue about are numerous it will be more correct to generalise them and then argue from the general idea, than to argue from one concrete object to another. But innumerable inferences are drawn from one particular thing to another, and these involve no generalisation.

Reason is chiefly the art of predicting by means of the intellect what will occur to us in the future. Its use is to enable us to prepare for future events in so far as our resources permit. We never predict quite accurately, but general preconceptions are better than none at all. The same process by which we preconceive the future can be applied to the conception of what is actually taking place but not within our ken —as at the antipodes—and can be applied also to events that took place in the past and will never be experienced by us. It might be objected that as regards the past we can have no motive in imagining it, seeing we can never experience it. But a conception of the past is often a necessary condition of our conceiving the future, and is artistically interesting. It awakens pleasing emotions to be able to picture to ourselves, even imperfectly, states of the world and of society that have long been obsolete.

An investigation of the manner in which reason supplies us with ideas of the unknown, involves the consideration and arrangement of so many details that it may be regarded as a small science in itself— DIALECTIC.

A dialectician (logician in the narrower sense) is neither a grammarian nor an encyclopedia of the best information on every subject. His office consists in deciding whether certain theorems are arguments or not. An ARGUMENT is an act or product of rational imagination. Theorems which purport to be arguments, but are not, are FALLACIES.

A fallacy is not merely a *bad* argument—it is no argument at all. Quite apart from fallacy there is a goodness and badness in arguments, but with this discrimination the dialectician (as such) has nothing to do. Only persons experienced in the matter are competent to decide between good and bad arguments. Hence when the quality of an argument is in question the dialectician takes no part in the debate: he is neither combatant nor umpire. He is at most an impartial president whose chief duty is to see that people do not debate about mere words and foregone conclusions. Granting that a theorem has the qualities of an argument, the dialectician is not competent to say that it is improper or too trivial to be discussed. He is not a judge of what people ought to be interested in.

From his better knowledge of what constitutes rational prediction, a dialectician may offer his services to disentangle and render explicit involved and partial arguments. Many people reason well who are yet unable to express themselves coherently. A dialectician should be able to reconstruct an argument from the slightest hint, as a naturalist imagines an animal from a single bone. In ordinary reasoning the arguments are seldom fully expressed, and the reasoners themselves are not always quite conscious of the premises from which they argue. All such suppressed and overlooked assumptions should be brought to light by dialectic, the aim of which is to render reason as self-conscious as possible.

Though a dialectician need not be an expert in any department of knowledge, he must know the facts on which an argument is built, otherwise he may be deceived by equivocal language. Reverting to the instance of the vase—the dialectician must have seen both the whole vase and the broken vase, but he need not have any opinion as to whether the proposed handle is the most suitable, or not. That must be left to those who are familiar with vases and who are interested in the restoration of the one in question.

The definition here given of the scope and office of dialectic may appear to some too modest. But in reality there is a great deal involved in it. Philosophers have been discussing Reason for twenty centuries or more, and have not produced a satisfactory definition of it. Consequently they cannot decide with any confidence whether a theorem is an argument or a fallacy. The cleverest of them give their sanction to theorems that are demonstrably fallacies.

They are evidently judging more by ear than by rule. All this causes confusion of mind and waste of energy.

Dialectic takes its general idea of reason from the higher analysis of logic, and brings the general idea to bear on concrete arguments. A dialectician makes a collection of theorems for study just as a botanist makes a collection of plants. He sorts them out into convenient classes, separates the valid or useful from the erroneous and misleading, studies the relation of language to argument and the influence for good or ill that words have upon rational thought.

From the example of the vase cited above it will be seen that in every act of reason two principal things are requisite. There must be something wholly known (or comparatively well known) and something less well known, and the reasoning or argument consists in ideally completing the latter on the model of the former. If we would predict the coming of a future season of the year we must have a picture in the mind of all the seasons in the order in which they occur. If we would go straight to a place on the surface of the earth we must have a plan of the way in our imagination. If we would predict the effect of a drug on an animal body we must have previously noticed the effect it has produced—and so on. Neither the mind nor intellect supplies spontaneously any of these models; they are all formed out of actual experience remembered and recollected. When they have been refined into extremely general ideas they are apt to be taken for innate tendencies of the intellect, as Kant erroneously thought. They are not so; all we know of the intellect is consistent with the belief that it begins with pure plasm without a trace of idea, and is absolutely indifferent to the imprints it may receive. Doctrines of innate ideas—innate forms of thought or categories —innate 'principles' of various kinds—are devices of metaphysicians to cover the weakness of their theories.

The two main parts of an argument divide naturally into four subdivisions. There is the thing argued about (corresponding to the broken vase); there is the ideal extension or restoration; in the model we reason from there are the parts corresponding to each of these. I propose to take terms for these four parts from one of the most important, formal and correct modes of reasoning—the application of a precedent or statute to a case in Law.

XVIII—THE RATIONAL PARALLEL

EVERY argument, whatever be the matter of it, consists in bringing a *Case* under a *Precedent*, and applying to the case ideally the better knowledge possessed of the precedent. The *Conclusion* (also called Inference or Deduction) is the result of this application, and is always an addition to our stock of ideas.

A conclusion has never the same reality as actual experience. It is not 'true' in that sense, though it may be 'morally' true, that is, we are ready to act upon it without hesitation—to stake our life or fortune on it. As regards actual or experienced fact there can be no argument, since it is useless to 'predict' what we already know.

Academical logicians have a doctrine the reverse of this. They assert that their syllogisms yield conclusions that are always as certain as the premises. Grant their premises and you are obliged to accept their conclusions. This is so, because a regular syllogistic conclusion is simply a restating in other words of the information, or part of the information, already contained in the premises. If the syllogism has any use at all, it is merely as an aid to recollection; no new idea is generated by it. It is needless to insist on a fact so notorious as that ordinary rational conclusions—those that form the staple of our daily thought—are not by any means so certain as the data from which they are drawn. For example, the sky is red and lowering this evening, and we conclude therefrom that the weather will be bad tomorrow. There is no doubt about the present aspect of the sky, but much doubt about the inference.

The form of an act of reasoning or argumentation may be rendered plainer by a diagram.

$$\frac{S}{C} \quad \frac{A}{I}$$

S A represents the precedent. S is the Subject or body of the precedent; A (the *Applicate*) is one property, or a part, or a relation of S abstracted from the rest to illustrate a case. C is the case; *I* is the conclusion (or inference). *I* results from imagining C to be associated with a property or relation similar to A. The sum of our *I*'s constitutes what we know of the world and man before we were born, of what is taking place in other parts of the world or universe, of what may take place in the future, and of the concealed and inaccessible parts of present objects. This is true not only of the results of our own reasoning but of what we have learned as verified knowledge from others, for the interpretation of language is, in the last analysis, a rational conclusion.

All the parts of an argument exist in the mind, but they are not always expressed in language. When treated dialectically the implicit members are expressed, and the terms arranged so as to show as clearly as possible the nature of the argument. The following are the points most necessary to be observed in constructing or analysing an argument.

(1) C must resemble S, for that is the basis of the argument. If C is not felt to be like S, or (as sometimes happens) is explicitly declared to be unlike S, there can be no conclusion. The precedent is not applicable to the case. A may, or may not, be associated with S; that is to say, a verbal negation may appear in the statement of the relation of S to A, but there must be no negation with respect to the relation of C to S.

The resemblance of C to S may, however, vary in degree from the faintest analogy to community of species. The difference between them may far outweigh their resemblance. There may even be no material likeness, but only a similarity of function, or position, or of any the most trivial attribute. Only it is to be observed that the kind and degree of resemblance between S and C determine the kind and degree of resemblance between A and *I*. We must not infer specifically unless the case is specifically like the precedent. In all other instances we can only infer proportionally or by transfusion.

(2) None of the antecedents must be a verbal or identical proposition, that is, a proposition which merely substitutes one name or nominal phrase for another; nor must the case be merely the precedent expressed in other words, or the precedent a paraphrase of the case. In any of these circumstances one of the elements of the argument is wanting; we have two names for one thing or two propositions giving the same information.

(3) The precedent may (as has been already remarked) be a general idea, or may be an individual idea or object. If S A has occurred frequently it is certain to be generalised, and so may form a maxim, a law, a rule, an induction, &c. But one well-observed precedent is enough to suggest a conclusion, if there has been no experience to the contrary. There is therefore no dialectical difference between arguing from a general idea (class notion) to an individual or subordinate idea, and arguing from one individual to another. Comparison and inference occur in both.

(4) After separating A from S care should be taken that it is A and not S that is used to generate I. Examples are plentiful of theorems in which S and A change parts, which invalidates the conclusion. Other errors in stating theorems intended to be

arguments will be noticed under the head of 'Fallacies.'

The following is an argument comformable to the above rules.

Tyrants	deserve death
Caesar was a tyrant	*no doubt he deserved death*

This square mode of stating the argument is adapted from the general type, and brings out the mutual relations of the compared parts better than the three-lined arrangement. The word 'therefore,' which usually introduces a logical conclusion, is ambiguous. It may mean that the antecedents are the causes of the fact mentioned in the conclusion, or merely that the antecedents are the reasons why we believe the conclusion. The former is the scientific 'therefore,' the latter is the purely dialectical. I shall generally omit the illative word, and print conclusions in italics, besides entering them invariably in the fourth compartment of the parallel when this arrangement is adopted.

An idea once generated in the intellect is not to be erased at pleasure. It can be obliterated only by the process of forgetting. If after we have formed a dialectical conclusion we meet with evidence that contradicts it, the only result of that evidence is to affix a mark of falsity to the conclusion, so that as often as it is recollected the stigma is recollected too, and neutralises the effect of the idea. A negative or destructive argument is thus, plasmically speaking, a positive addition to the idea it seeks to efface. For the time being it renders the idea more conspicuous, as the word CANCELLED stamped in large letters across a document makes it more evident than it was before; but no doubt the stigmatising of an idea hastens the process of oblivion, for we thenceforth bestow less attention upon it. Stigmatic arguments are not another species, but merely the ordinary constructive arguments used for a particular purpose.

Suppose we have inferred from the general resemblance of the earth to the moon that the latter is inhabited, we stigmatise this belief by such an argument as—

Without air	animals cannot live
There is no air in the moon	*there can be no life in the moon*

There is an exception to the rule that argument is superfluous when the speaker has already verified the conclusion. It is when he is addressing a person who has not had the same experience as himself and who doubts his word. The speaker may then resort to arguments drawn from antecedents recognised by the hearer, if any such are applicable to the subject. But a fact may be truly reported though neither the witness nor a sceptical hearer can find dialectical antecedents to prove it, for there may be no relation between the fact in question and any prior knowledge they possess, or they may not be able to find the relation.

This brings us again to that view of the intellect which represents it as artificial and limited by experience. Man is rational only on matters familiar to him; in utterly novel circumstances he is irrational, and must fall back for guidance on his general mental sentiment, or the advice of persons more experienced than himself.

XIX—HYPOTHETICAL ARGUMENTS

It is allowable to imagine ourselves placed in circumstances not yet realised, or in possession of information not yet acquired, and to anticipate or rehearse the reasoning we should employ under the supposed conditions. Such arguments take in language a conditional or hypothetical phraseology.

The case may be entirely fictitious, but I cannot find a valid instance of a whole precedent being fictitious. Its dubiety turns on our knowledge or ignorance of the applicate. Has a subject such or such an attribute? Then it may be applied to illustrate a certain case. 'If it is true that Damon and Pythias are inseparable, then *Pythias must be in town*, for I have just seen Damon.'

It is more often the case that is dubious. 'If Caius is a European *he is white*, for all Europeans are white.' 'If Damon is in town *Pythias is in town*, for they are inseparable.' 'If I were you *I should defer the voyage to the summer season*, as I have always found winter travelling disagreeable.' But the word 'if' does not always mark a hypothetical thought. In the proposition, 'if children are neglected they will grow up ignorant,' we have a dogmatic or assertorial judgment—'neglected children grow up ignorant.' (Bain.)

The precedent may be suppressed in hypothetical as in dogmatic argument. 'If the crops are good, corn will be cheap' implies the unspoken precedent, 'good crops have been invariably followed by cheap corn.' 'If logic is useless it deserves to be neglected,' carries the mind to the more general thesis, 'all useless studies deserve to be neglected.' 'If Great Britain should be invaded the volunteers will be called out,' rests on the precedent judgment, 'it is the duty of the volunteer army to repel invaders.'

Arguments in which both applicate and case are hypothetical are so very dubious that they cannot be considered of any practical use. '*If* opium is poisonous, and *if* this substance is opium, you will be poisoned by taking this substance.'

The Aristotelian hypothetical is almost invariably a fallacy, sometimes on more than one account. It usually consists of—first, a conditional or doubtful statement; next, a solution of the doubt by means of positive information; finally and by way of inference the first statement is given without the doubt. Here is an example from Jevons: 'If the barometer is falling, bad weather is coming; but the barometer is falling; therefore bad weather is coming.'

Where did the information that the barometer is falling come from? If we knew it before uttering the first proposition, we were affecting an ignorance that did not exist. The second proposition takes away all occasion for argument; it is an amendment of the first proposition, and what we get from the theorem as a whole is a *case*, followed by a prediction for which there is no precedent justification. We are arguing in a circle.

'If Aristotle is right, slavery is a proper form of society; but slavery is not a proper form of society; therefore Aristotle is not right.' If we knew for certain (as the second proposition indicates) that slavery is not a proper form of society, what is the use or meaning of treating the question as hypothetical (as is done in the first)? If we acquired the information after uttering the first proposition, there was no occasion to go on with the argument; we should have said simply, 'Slavery is not a proper form of society, though Aristotle said it was.' It is needless, except for verbal completeness, to say 'he was not right'—we have *logically* said so.

When two or more alternative data are presented, of which only one is valid or relevant to a proposed argument, but we know not at first which the valid datum is, we have the *dilemma (trilemma, tetralemma,* &c.) of logicians. In such conditions we have a double process to go through; we must first settle by observation or by an auxiliary argument which of the alternative data to select, and then work out the principal argument in the regular dogmatic form.

Suppose we have to determine dialectically the specific gravity of a piece of metal, but do not know whether it is gold or gun-metal. It is evident we must first somehow make up our mind as to its identity, and then proceed on the usual method of argumentation. The 'making up our mind' is probably itself an argument, and might be of this character— 'A piece of yellow metal stamped with what appears to be a hall-mark, is more likely to be gold than gun-metal; this piece of metal has traces of such a stamp; so I conclude *it is gold.*' Then we proceed to the principal question—'The specific gravity of gold is 19.26; I have concluded that this object is gold; I conclude further that *it has a specific gravity of* 19.26.'

We may work out all the alternative conclusions first and fix on a datum afterwards, as in deciding how we shall invest our money. 'If I put my money in Consols I shall have a small return with good security; if I buy Patagonian bonds I may have a large interest for a time, but the security is bad.' The next thing to settle is whether in our experience or on accepted principles small profit with good security is, or is not, to be preferred to large profit and bad security: having decided in favour of the former alternative, we now choose our investment dogmatically—'A good security with small profit is to be preferred; Consols are of this character; *they are a suitable investment for me.*'

We may be unable to decide for any of the alternative data, but we work out all the possible arguments as hypotheses, and so are prepared in a degree for all the possible events. A person is seen approaching our residence, but we cannot discern whether it is A. B., who is a bore, or C. D., who is an entertaining companion. We argue rapidly—'If it is A.B. *I shall have a bad half-hour*, for he always wearies me; if it is C. D. *I shall have an agreeable distraction*, for he is very amusing.'

According to the syllogists, the dilemmatic premises are a statement of alternative data and the choice of one of them, and the inference is the rejection of the remainder: or the rejection may be given as matter of fact and the selection as conclusion. In neither case have we argument.

From the moment we select a datum the remaining data are of no import to us, and they need not be mentioned. The selection of one datum is logically identical with the rejection of the rest, and this is therefore not a conclusion from that.—' Do you take tea or coffee?'—'Tea, please.'—'Then I conclude you do not take coffee.'—A person who would 'conclude' in this fashion would be justly deemed irrational. The choice of the tea is a fact, and the rejection of the coffee is the same fact otherwise expressed, so that the rejection cannot be a rational conclusion.—' My doctor sends me off every winter to Nice, Algiers, or Egypt; but I never go to Algiers or Egypt.'—There is no occasion to say, 'therefore you go to Nice'; that has been already announced as a matter of fact and is not susceptible of inference. For the sake of verbal emphasis we might remark, ' So it is to Nice you go', but this is not logically requisite.

Whately's examples of this kind of theorem are exactly of the model just given.—'Either the earth is eternal, or the work of chance, or the work of an intelligent Being; it is not eternal, nor the work of chance, *therefore* it is the work of an intelligent Being.' This is put forward in all gravity as a specimen of reasoning. It is plain that if we know the premises as matters of fact, we also know the proposed conclusion as a matter of fact. There is no occasion to reason about it.

The Aristotelian hypothetical can be reduced to arithmetical subtraction. Suppose we put five balls into a bag and afterwards take out three without seeing the remainder : is the judgment that two balls remain in the bag a logical inference? No—it is matter of fact. Since we last perceived the objects they have undergone diminution, but that does not confer on what is left of them the imaginary character proper to a rational conclusion. What remains is as much fact —recollected but not imaginary fact—as before the subtraction.

Whately's next example is—'It is either spring, summer, autumn, or winter ; but it is neither spring nor summer ; therefore it is either autumn or winter.' This is aggravated fallacy. Not only is it mere subtraction, but the remainder is *perceived*—not recollected, as in the preceding case. The actual season of the year is a known fact, and is not rendered more certain by an inference drawn from the absence of some other season. Arguments have no validity as against matters of fact, and add nothing to their authority. Fact is above, and independent of, argument. The example just cited may be paralleled thus—'The cards in my hand are either spades, hearts, clubs, or diamonds ; but they are neither spades nor hearts ; therefore they are either clubs or diamonds'.—I *see* that they are either clubs or diamonds : the perceptual judgment renders the rational

—imaginary—judgment superfluous. Reason is intended to supplement experience—not to supersede it.

XX—DEBATE

The purpose of debate is to determine the goodness or badness of an argument by general logical criticism and knowledge of the matter. This is not dialectic, but takes place after the dialectician has declared that a given theorem is valid argument. If then its conclusion is repugnant to us we may seek to stigmatise it—or remove a stigma as the case may be—by going behind the argument to the composition of the judgments that enter into it.

Let us take the case of Caesar being proved to be a tyrant in a society that punishes tyranny with death. There are two ways in which he may be saved or his punishment mitigated.

We are not bound to take the first precedent that is offered from which to generate a conclusion. We grant that Caesar resembles the general notion 'tyrant,' but we ask if he does not resemble in an equal or greater degree some other person or class in regard to whom capital punishment is no just treatment. Does he resemble a 'successful and patriotic general'—a 'benevolent monarch'— a 'wise legislator'—a 'virtuous man'? All these resemblances are compatible with his being a tyrant in some senses of the word. Let us not condemn Caesar for what may be a merely technical offence—the usurpation of authority—if in other respects he is an admirable man. So an opportunity must be given to Caesar or his advocate to suggest other precedents, yielding a different conclusion, by which to complete our imperfect knowledge of the case. Socrates, when he was brought under the class 'perverters of youth'—which also yielded the conclusion 'death'—suggested as an amendment that he should be classed under 'national benefactors,' with the conclusion 'maintenance for life at the public expense.'

It is not enough that we can say of a case that it 'is' this or that, and so proceed to draw the conclusion bound up in that classification. 'Is' in the case means likeness to the precedent, and one 'is' is good only when no better can be found.

If after having weighed the alternative precedents it appears clear that Caesar resembles tyrants more than any other class of persons, the prospect looks bad for him. But there is still a chance of escaping the worst penalty. It turns on the meaning of the word 'all,' which in logic generally introduces a proposition to which no exception has been found—the misnamed and misleading 'universal.'

Logicians do not hesitate to say that in this connection it means 'all possible, known or unknown, past or future individuals of the class.' They suppose, or talk as if they supposed, that at some fixed date in our life we enter into possession of our general ideas, and that no subsequent experience can modify them. Hence the moment it is admitted that Caesar is a tyrant, he is supposed to come under the rule of a stereotyped general idea with inflexible consequences.

This is not quite so. 'All' does not mean 'all possible' but 'all known up to the present time, *exclusive of the case under discussion.*' Our general or average ideas are the plasmic product of the individuals we have actually known—not a unit more. And as that idea is liable to be modified by every new individual examined, it is possible that on examining Caesar we may find reason to change our general idea, to the extent at least of dividing it into two species, the tyrants who deserve death and the tyrants who deserve some milder punishment, and that we shall resolve to bring Caesar under the latter species. Thus if the idea threatens to hang Caesar, on the other hand Caesar may burst the idea, and his case establish itself as a new precedent. That is how general ideas multiply—by a sort of fission.

In the proposition 'tyrants deserve death' as first proposed, we are dealing with the old general idea, and—as regards all individuals except those from which it was drawn—the proposition is little more than a hypothesis. The idea is itself on trial. Until Caesar is examined we do not fully know how the general tyrant is in future to be defined. Our examination of Caesar is a part of our education on the subject of tyrants. In judging we learn, and the general idea which remains *after Caesar is examined* is that by which he is to be judged.

If our idea of tyrant remains unshaken after the trial of Caesar, and if he is found to resemble that class more than any other, then—and not till then—are we compelled to pass on him the judgment associated with the definition of tyrant.

An argument based on a particular or solitary precedent is criticised on the same principles. We seek to prove either that the case is not sufficiently like the precedent to justify the application, or that the applicate is not a property of the precedent. If we make good either of these propositions, we prevent the suggested conclusion from being fastened on the case.

The syllogistic dialecticians do not admit alternative precedents or reconstruction of general ideas: their terms and figures are not adapted to express such notions. Hence they cannot evade a conclusion whose premises are correctly given. They have an axiom to the effect that a judgment must be absolutely true or absolutely false—a door must be open or shut, it cannot be ajar; every colour is white or black, it cannot be green or grey, and so on. Now in practical reasoning we may and constantly do admit premises and reject the conclusions they dialectically involve. We look at the question 'from another point of view.' This means that while admitting there is some ground for bringing a case under a certain precedent, we contend that on the whole it is preferable to bring it under another precedent with a different conclusion. The proposed handle *may* fit the vase somehow, but we think another sort of handle will suit it better. Or—rather than accept an objectionable conclusion—we will divide our idea. This is degree in truth. And that is the elastic method on which we reason in actual affairs. Logicians give a false account of reason, and so their systems are neglected and their authority is never recognised in real debates.

CATEGORIES

XXI—CATEGORIES OF SUBSTANTIALISM, AND OTHERS

A CATEGORY is primarily a class of Judgments. Since arguments are composed of judgments, a category is also a class of arguments; that is to say, the argument follows the classification of the judgment. This is not the practice of syllogists, who have categories for judgments only, the arguments being classified according to verbal expression.

I distinguish six categories—two Natural and four Artificial. The judgments of a natural category concern experience presented in a synthesis whose composition is due to the noumenal mind; the categories corresponding to this definition are—

Inherence—
Association.

An artificial category is so called because the synthesis is formed by the subjective mind.

The first category of this kind is

Perspection—

which is an artificial arrangement of objects according

to a figurative interpretation of certain appearances they present.

The second artificial category I will call

Concretion—

as it is an ideal cohesion of experiences never wholly perceived at once. These two categories are those chiefly responsible for the realistic mode of thought.

The third artificial category is that which is called in science causation, but it is only

Sequence,—

that is, a series of phenomena sufficiently coherent to afford a basis for inference, but not necessarily or energically connected. Hume and others have conclusively proved that such phenomena are not causally related.

Finally there is

Causation—

in the proper sense of the word, that is, the relation between energic mind and its effects. This is the category of human affairs generally, and of all the Cosmic that we explain by analogy with the Human. It is the only exhaustive explanation of phenomena, and so is the category which philosophy would substitute for the rest. When we can truly resolve things into effects analogous to human actions, we have reached the highest standpoint from which they can be viewed. *Realistic* anthropomorphism is the first and rudest explanation of things: *idealistic* anthropomorphism is the last and most refined.

The artificial categories are all formed on analogies supplied by the natural, since the intellect is incapable of imagining anything absolutely original.

Each category may include judgments of other categories in a subordinate relation. Inherence and concretion enter to some extent as auxiliaries into all the others. A group category may be treated as an individual object for certain purposes, and an individual as a group of properties. In the one case a fictitious unity is created, in the other a real unity is imaginatively dissolved. But in general the categories are sufficiently distinct and may be considered as mutually exclusive. They will be separately analysed and exemplified.

The term category is used in common logic to signify the final classes into which *judgments* can be arranged. To this minor use only is the category applied. It does not either denote a classification of *arguments* or a distinct province of ideas whose origin and validity should be a matter of investigation. In Greek and modern logic arguments are distinguished solely by their verbal expression—never by the character of the judgment that enters into them. Treated in this superficial and haphazard way, the categories necessarily play a quite insignificant part in philosophy.

The oldest known set of categories is that quoted

by Aristotle in his Metaphysic as being held by a sect of Pythagoreans. It consists of the following series of contraries—

Bound.	Infinity.	Rest.	Motion.
Odd.	Even.	Straight.	Crooked.
Unity.	Plurality.	Light.	Darkness.
Right.	Left.	Good.	Bad.
Male.	Female.	Square.	Oblong.

Aristotle's own categories are the following:—

(1) *Essence* or *Substance*, as man, horse:

(2) *Quantity*, as two cubits long:

(3) *Quality*, as white, erudite:

(4) *Relation*, as double, half, greater:

(5) *Place*, as in the Agora:

(6) *Time*, as yesterday:

(7) *Posture*, as standing, sitting:

(8) *Having* (Condition?), as to be shod, armed:

(9) *Action*, as he is cutting, burning:

(10) *Passion*, as he is being cut.

This list can be reduced to one half the number. Quantity, Quality, Posture, Condition are kinds of *Attribute* or *Property* of the Substance. Place and Time are valid. Action and Passion are both referable to causation. Non-causal sequence or consecution (as day following night)—one of the commonest judgments—is not mentioned.

The Stoics reduced Aristotle's ten categories to

four—Substratum or Substance, the Essential Quality, Manner of being, and Relation.

Kaṇáda, a Hindu philosopher, has six categories—Substance, Quality, Action, Genus, Individuality, and Concretion or Co-inherence.

Plotinus was acquainted with the Aristotelian and Stoic lists and offers as his own :—(1) Fundamental forms of the *Ideal*—Being, Rest, Motion, Identity, Difference ; (2) Categories of the *Sensible*—Substance, Relation, Quality, Quantity, Motion.

Descartes recognised but two final categories, the Absolute and the Relative.

Kant has an elaborate scheme of categories, which he considered to be, not merely classes of judgments, but innate power of the mind by which we are moved to form the judgments. They are the following :—

I. *Of Quantity*.	Unity, Plurality, Totality.	
II. *Of Quality*.	Reality, Negation, Limitation.	
III. *Of Relation*.	Of Inherence and Subsistence (*substantia et accidens*).	
	Of Causality and Dependence (cause and effect).	
	Of Community (reciprocity between the active and the passive).	
IV. *Of Modality*.	Possibility, Impossibility, Existence, Non-existence, Necessity, Contingency.	

Sir William Hamilton's categories were Being, Being by itself, and Being by accident.

Categories have also been proposed by Spinoza, Locke, Wolff, Leibnitz, Herbart, Mill, and others. No two of them are alike. They are not formed on any definite principle, but are individual opinions as to the most convenient way to classify judgments [1].

XXII—INHERENCE

An object being given by perception we develop our knowledge of it, first by narrowing our focus of attention so as to perceive parts and single attributes of the object; next by widening our attention so as to include several objects in one view. The first process is Analysis or Abstraction; it informs us what attributes co-inhere to constitute the object. The second is Synthesis or Grouping, by which we learn the relations of one thing to others. These operations comprise all we know about a thing, for it can have no attributes which are not either internal or external.

[1] Ueberweg's *Logic*, Fleming's *Vocabulary*, and Dickenson's *Dict. of Philosophy*.

Practical analysis means cutting a thing to pieces or dissolving it, and this has a certain value because it multiplies objects. But it does not increase our knowledge of the first thing. On the contrary, by destroying a thing we render a knowledge of it impossible. The analysis which gives knowledge is Metaphysical Abstraction—an attention concentrated on the parts of a thing without destroying their connection with the other inherent parts. The metaphysical elements may be quite different from the mechanically divisible parts. They are generally a species of things which could not exist alone, such as red, blue, straight, curved, square, round, acid, sweet, insipid, fragrant, sharp, hot, heavy, dull, loud, bright, and a multitude of properties of that abstract kind.

For many of these—at least for the description of them—a comparison of two or more things is essential. A sound is heard to be loud by comparison with another which is low or soft; a knife is known to be blunt by experience of another more sharp, or the same knife in a sharper condition. But comparison does not alter the essential character of abstract attention—it serves merely as an incitement to it. Difference between qualities otherwise alike whets our attention to a finer discrimination.

The properties recognised by each sense are easily distinguished in the bulk from those of another sense.

Colour is distinct from Figure in a more marked degree than red from blue or square from circular. Fine degrees of Sound may be difficult to discriminate, but not the difference between a sound and a smell or a taste.

Still broader contrasts give rise to an artificial but sometimes useful kind of attribution—the negative. When we do not know much concerning the positive characteristics of a thing, it is something to know that it has *not* this or that property. What Thought is, positively, few people know, but they are able to say (with a little prompting) that it is un-extended, im-material, im-ponderable, and so forth. This comparison re-acts on the thing better known, and so we call visual objects 'extended' from their dissimilarity to thoughts. But for that there would have been no occasion to notice the abstract extension of visual objects. The term 'visual object' would have tacitly included extension. There must be great and general ignorance of a thing to excuse the negative attribution: it is not allowable to speak of plants as non-metals, or sheep as non-horses, but a large class of animals is called in-vertebrate. In this case the negative property serves to bar a possible inference that all animals are vertebrate, since those we know best are so.

The judgment in this category is a consciousness of the attributes making up a thing, or so much of it as interests us. 'Cleopatra's Needle is an obelisk of granite, about sixty-eight feet high, and is carved with hieroglyphics.' If we go on to say that it stands on the Thames Embankment, we shift into the category of association. The relation of an object to its place is different from that of one inherent attribute of the object to another, or to the whole.

The properties of a general idea are defined in this category. The synthesis is natural or noumenal, the artificiality of the idea consisting merely in the omission of some of the concrete properties. 'Garden rhubarb [in general] has broadly cordate leaves, strongly veined beneath; the footstalks are long, thick, and fleshy, with a channel above; its growth is exceedingly rapid.' These are properties inherent in a unity not of our making. The botanist changes into the category of sequence when he says, 'the stalks are used for tarts and made into jam.'

In a complicated object or general idea some of the judgments we treat as inherent may be inferences in other categories used subordinately. 'The ancient Persians had remarkably thin and weak skulls. They were good horsemen and archers, courageous and spirited in battle. They wore a tunic and trousers of leather . . . They were quick and lively, keen-witted, capable of repartee, ingenious, and—for Orientals—far-sighted. They had fancy and imagination, a relish for poetry and art, and they were not without a certain power of political combination.' Some of these properties might have been perceived objectively, but not the possession of fancy and imagination, which could only be known by inference in causation—here used to complete a coherent unity. The historian employs causation as a principal category when he tells us that 'their bards did not touch the chords which rouse what is noblest and highest in our nature.' The thought implied in touching chords—the notion of will directing action—is a different judgment from the perception of an inherent permanent attribute.

The argument in this category consists in ideally completing an imperfect object by comparison with a similar object, or the idea of a similar object. Suppose we have studied thoroughly one or more rhubarb plants, and then see a plant with broadly cordate leaves, footstalks long, thick, and fleshy, and having a channel above. In the time at our disposal we cannot ascertain if its growth is exceedingly rapid, but we are justified in inferring that it is, and that the plant we are examining is in all other respects rhubarb. If the Egyptian obelisks we have seen were sculptured with hieroglyphics throughout their length, and we see an obelisk part of which is underground, it is a rational inference that that part also is sculptured.

We have proved that certain samples of aluminium have a specific gravity of 2·6, and then see a metal—of specific gravity unknown—which has all the other properties of aluminium: we may confidently infer that this metal also would, if tested, show a specific gravity of 2·6.

For purposes of reason it may be necessary to compare things that cannot be brought physically together. When this happens we generally compare them in *idea*, or the idea of one with the other as object. When great accuracy is required and the idea —which is always rather vague—cannot be relied on, we have recourse to mediate comparison. *Standards* are employed. These are manageable or portable objects with which principal things are separately compared by way of effecting indirectly a comparison between them. Standards can only mediate comparisons between *abstract* properties, for if they contained all the concrete properties of the compared objects they would, by supposition, be as unmanageable as the latter. We have standards for length in rules, scales, tapes, chains; the balance is a standard for weight. There are also scales for pitch of sound, varieties of colour, degree of light, heat, atmospheric pressure, and probably some others for special purposes.

Indirect comparison is not in itself inference; or if inference it is subordinate and preparatory to some more important conclusion. A coin is weighed and concluded to be *light*, but this is only a datum in determining the more important question whether it is a forged coin or not.

XXIII—ASSOCIATION

In this category we widen the attention so as to include several objects in one act of perception.

The first result of this diffusion of attention is to lessen the brilliancy of objects. Our attention is a light which is intensified when narrowed and concentrated—enfeebled when dispersed over several objects. The observation of a group amounts practically to observing the objects in rapid succession. At a given moment we perceive only one thing well, or it may be only a small part of a thing, but we have a dull sense of other things adjacent, which we have just seen and may immediately see again in any order we please. That is all that is meant by perception of a group.

To distinguish this category properly from the next we must consider the group of objects as divested of depth or distance outwards. It is to be regarded as a flat surface standing a few feet from us, the objects in it having absolutely the dimensions they appear to have. This is in fact their *real* magnitude, for the supposed real magnitude is a matter of theory, and means the perceptual magnitude taken under certain conditions of observation. The real magnitude is constantly changing, so for practical convenience in determining size, etc., we refer all objects to one condition of observation—that in which they can be touched as well as seen.

In metaphysic we are not obliged to recognise this convention. If an object a mile off appears to be an inch high, it is an inch high as really as if it were in a photograph or picture and materially represented of that height. The mystery of the change of size in objects is not explained or reasoned away by any device for overcoming some of its practical inconveniences. It depends on the degree of energy with which minds affect each other.

A group has properties which an object has not; or, if this be not strictly the case, we may say that the properties we look for in a group are not those we distinguish in a single object. The special properties of a group are *positions*. It is unnecessary to say 'relative' positions, for position cannot be otherwise than relative. Position cannot be defined by reference to anything more simple. What is meant is intuitively known to everybody. But let us take a concrete example—a man with a horse and cart standing on a bridge. Each object in this group has a position towards the other objects. The bridge is *over* the river and *under* the cart; the cart is *upon* the bridge and *behind* the horse; the man is *in* the cart; the horse is *before* and *outside* of the cart, it is *near* one end of the bridge, *far* from the other, and *between* the two extremities. These are the principal positions in a natural group or association, by which is meant the objects we can see (or are supposed to see) simultaneously, and whose mutual positions we are considering.

The use of observing positions is the same as that which moves us to all rational study, namely, its value in prediction. We can reason from one object to another in a group just as we reason from one property to another in an object.

Suppose our perception of a landscape is interrupted for a moment, and when we next endeavour to perceive it we find we only perceive a portion of it, the rest being 'hidden' by an intervening object. As far as we are concerned the hidden part has been annihilated. We only remember what was there. But this recollection is also a preconception of what we may be able to cause to appear again, either by removing the obstructing object, by waiting till it has been removed, or by walking round and standing between it and the landscape.

If this be too close to mere recollection, we have pure reasoning when from the general appearance of a group we imagine generally some concealed part of it not before seen. A procession of people dressed in mourning is usually accompanied by a hearse: from perceiving the people only on a certain occasion we predict the hearse. The sound of a steam-whistle enables us to imagine a train in a certain locality, though fog or other obstruction may prevent our seeing it. The scent of flowers prepares us for finding them somewhere near us. From smoke we predict the nearness of a chimney. The trail of an animal is a clue to his position.

The judgment in this category is therefore a consciousness of position, such as those mentioned above. The argument is a completion of one association by comparison with another—the expectation of similarity in groups.

Movement. All judgments as to *change* of position in objects come under this category. It takes at least two things arranged in a group to produce the perception of movement. If there were but one thing in our field of observation we could not say whether it moved or not, for there would be nothing which it would pass, or leave, or approach. It would appear to stand still. There is, however, more in movement than depends on mere perception.

All movement is due to energy either in the observer or in the other mind acting upon his. Energy is not a generalisation of moving things, nor a property, nor a relation, though all these may be signs of energy. The most abstract idea of movement is *Motion*. It may be defined as a series of positions.

Number. If we treat a group as a large loose object we shall perceive in it certain properties not strictly positional. Number is one of these.

A group of three coins has not the same practical value as a group of six or sixty, and we are thus obliged to notice the difference and distinguish degrees of this property by names—hence Arithmetic.

Flat Space or space of two dimensions is another property of a group. Grouped objects have frequently intervals between them. Such intervals are negations of perception—interruptions or discontinuities of experience. But by abstraction we can reduce the objects bounding an interval to a geometrical line, and so give a sort of positive existence to the interval. Thus we talk of a hole or of darkness as if they were true objects, and measure them by standards of length.

If we abstract the boundary lines from a space we get the idea 'intervalness,' which is the right name for two-dimensioned space. This abstract idea is nearly the same as abstract size. Space is interval without bounds—size is object without contents. Space and size are equally *nothing* intrinsically or in their own right, but they have been reached by different modes of refining away the positive qualities associated with them, and this difference of origin is slightly suggested by their names. Spaces have a use in perception similar to *rests* in music—they relieve the attention and give contrast and vigour to the next positive object.

XXIV—PERSPECTION

THIS is the first of the artificial categories. It is an ideal treatment of an associated group to facilitate a certain kind of reasoning.

Reason—let me repeat—is the imaginary extension of experience by comparison with more complete experience of a similar kind. By reasoning in inherence we complete single objects; by inference in association we complete groups. These two categories demonstrate that a natural group consists of fragments of objects, and fragments of other natural groups which are possible but not yet developed. A hill is partly concealed by a house, the house partly concealed by a tree, the tree by a stone fence, the fence by a growth of ivy. A river disappears at a curve and is lost to view; we know from experience of other rivers that under certain conditions we might perceive the river further on as a feature in several more landscapes. As we gaze at an association of objects these possible completions occur to us—not fully or definitely but sufficiently to convince us that the group might be developed into many other groups, and into a multitude of objects of forms different from those we actually perceive. By our hypothesis the observer has always been stationary, the objects have moved to and fro but not from near to far. Their real dimensions have remained unaltered, and nothing has occurred to suggest that they ever appear of other dimensions. In short we are gazing on a piece of stage-scenery.

But there is another element in perception. We and all other real (mental) beings are part of the cosmic force. We are co-creators of what we perceive—limited gods, not machine-men as the scientific people would have us believe. But for our power of affecting each other and our readiness to receive impressions from other minds, there would be no perception—no material objects. We (that is, all sentient beings) could, by unanimous resolution, annul the material creation—blot out the universe of objective things in a moment. United to and implied in this general power is the particular power of modifying our world without destroying it. We can redistribute the active and passive forces so as to produce other perceptual effects than those present at a given moment. And we habitually do this to some extent. Within a limited scope our world is plastic as dough, and we knead it to any form we please. For example, we exert energy to change our place, and immediately the group before us breaks up and undergoes metamorphosis. Some objects disappear altogether, and entirely new objects present themselves. Some become smaller, others larger; some fractional forms fill out to completion, some integers undergo curtailment, others separate into several distinct objects. In a few minutes the first group has dissolved into a second, which may merge into a third, and so on indefinitely.

In contemplating these phenomena we discern a third form of completeness and incompleteness, distinct from those that enter into inherence and association. Hence a new type of reasoning—another category: the Perspective.

It will be convenient to suppose that the modifications to which it refers are solely due to the observing mind, as the most conspicuous and comprehensive really are, but some of the minor perspective changes are due to the noumenon of the object.

We have first to get a criterion of perspective perfection. What this shall be is to some extent a matter of convention. The standard I shall adopt is, that an object of a nature to be perceptible to all the senses would be most perfect if within reach of touch. If it can be heard it is then heard at its loudest—this is correct enough for our purpose,—if it can be seen it is then seen at its largest and brightest. This is Perspective Completeness at the Tactual Range. It means the closest contact of noumenon and subject, compatible with clear definition in perception.

Now let us exert energy and disarrange a group. Those things that were or might have been tangible in the former position, are no longer so, but they may still be seen, heard, or even smelt. The bright colours have however somewhat faded, the size has shrunk, some of the details are lost. Here is a lapse from perspective completeness. It is indicated, not as in the first two categories by mechanical cutting away of mass and circumstance, but by deterioration all over the object. We seem to be thrown out of focus in relation to it, and the perspective degradation may increase until the object has dwindled to a speck and finally disappears altogether.

The judgment in this category consists in observing the kind and degree of degradation to which things are liable in perspective. In addition to change in size, brightness, detail and loudness, which have been already mentioned, occultation as in the second category can be used as an indirect datum. An object which eclipses another is invariably more perfect perspectively than the object eclipsed. The motion of objects has also to be taken into account. As objects degrade their movements slacken, and recover power as the objects are restored.

By attending to all these indications and checking each by the rest, we have the elements of a fairly accurate inference as to comparative perspective condition. We have constant practice in this sort of thought with frequent opportunities of verifying our conclusions; penalties are annexed to failure and rewards to success. It is no wonder then that in the course of years we become expert in judging of perspective condition, so that when confronted with a natural group we can estimate almost instantly the degree in which each object falls short of perspective integrity.

The result of this practice is that on perceiving a natural group of many objects, we graduate them according to the perspective deterioration which each exhibits, and for greater precision we figure the perspective difference as an interval between the objects —an imaginary interval modelled on the true interval of association. The object on a distant horizon is visually as near as the ground we can touch by stooping, but in this imaginary group the former is placed at the far end of the line and the latter at the near end, and between them are ranged the other objects each at a point corresponding to what we suppose to be its perspective distance. That is how a landscape acquires depth. Space outwards is an ideal imitation of real lateral interval. It is the measure and expression of perspective defacement.

From what has been said it follows that the near objects will be relatively large, clear, and lively in motion, while the far will be small, dull, and slow, but this rule is liable to many exceptions which can only be learnt by experience.

On the analogy of the other forms of inference—which consist in completing imperfect things by reference to others more perfect—the essence of an argument in perspective is the power to imagine an object which is perspectively defective, brought up to the tactual range and displaying all the qualities it would possess in that position. This is done by comparing it with the idea of the same or a similar object experienced at the tactual range; and is done for an ulterior purpose, like all other intellectual operations. A great part of our material happiness consists in the exercise of the short senses (taste, touch and smell), and the chief use of perspective reasoning is to enable us to judge of the energy required to bring a distant object near for close perception. We have therefore to observe our energic fluctuations in conjunction with perspective change, if we would extract the utmost practical benefit from this category. The perspective inferences are none the less useful after we discover that they are not intuitions, and that the completeness we imaginatively assign to distant objects has no existence until we exert the corresponding energy.

A landscape being rendered perspective we can determine the perspective state of any new object that may enter it, by reference to the objects adjoining it, and this though the object be of a species quite unknown to us and which therefore, by itself, would afford no clue to its perspective distance.

The imaginary interval we place between objects of different perspective effacement, can be expressed in terms of exact lateral measurement. This is done by developing and measuring the associative groups represented in the perspective group. Supposing we wish to get an exact definition of the perspective condition of a mountain relative to a certain station, we can, from that station, develop all the natural groups up to the mountain (walk over the ground) and measure the lateral intervals and masses disclosed. The total measurements will be a definition of the mountain's perspective distance in terms of true associative distance. That is what we mean by saying a mountain is ten miles off. It is not *really* ten miles off—it is not an inch off. But to render it tactually perfect we should have to expend an amount of energy equal to 17,600 times the energy required to move from one associative object to another a yard apart from it laterally. If we practise the mileage scale in conjunction with the perspective indications, we may acquire the art of expressing in miles, though not measured, the distance of objects estimated from purely perspective data, but few can do this with any near approach to exactness [1].

The realistic three-dimensioned space is a combination of the true interval of association and the false interval of perspective. This generates an idea resembling the capacity or vacancy in a room or vessel, and thus it is supposed that objects occupy a sort of universal room without walls, floor, or ceiling. It is however the enclosing objects which make a room,. and when they are abstracted there remains nothing. The universal room is therefore nothing—a myth. It is a useful working theory for common purposes, but in philosophy it is superfluous and obstructive.

[1] When the perspective object is accurately measured by instrument at a known distance from the eye, and the tactual size of the object is also known, the associative distance can be calculated by simple proportion. Multiply the measuring distance by the tactual size and divide the product by the perspective size—the quotient is the distance. The perspective size of objects is greatly exaggerated in realism. Most people think they see a man at his full stature for a distance of fifty yards or so. At that distance the tallest man does not measure half an inch in height. At twenty feet a six-foot man measures 3.6 inches—at ten feet 7.2 inches. The people assembled in a room forty feet long range in real—perspective—height from seven inches to two inches. When a man is nearer than ten feet we do not perceive him in one operation—we observe him in parts which we put together in the mind.

In the definitions of geometry no difference is made between the depth of a landscape and the 'third dimension' of any small cubic object. They are both called 'third dimension' or 'cubic dimension.' Yet they are inferences of different categories, and neither is real. The former, as we have just seen, is the imagined redintegration of objects perspectively shrunk and defaced. The latter is the imaginary completion of a thing having many surfaces or facets, only one of which can be shown at a time.

Sky Perspection. The effect produced on our mind by the observation of celestial objects, reveals at once the artificiality of cubic space. Clouds in their form and movements are somewhat like earthly things—vapour or mountains,—and so we conceive them partially graduated in distance and floating in a concavity. But whether they are a mile off, or twenty miles off, few of us can tell.

When we contemplate the sun, moon and stars, our realism is completely at fault. These we cannot modify at will, and they move too slowly and present too uniform an aspect to cause the perspective effect. Since we have never seen them at the tactual range we know not to what degree they are perspectively incomplete; hence they appear without relative distance—distance being simply a metaphor of perspective effacement. If 'cubic space' is real, let the realists tell us why we do not see it in the sky—why we do not arrange the stars behind each other according to their calculated distances. This question is unanswerable realistically, but idealistically it presents no difficulty. The sky is not spaced, because the conditions are wanting under which the illusion of terrestrial space is formed in the intellect.

By close instrumental attention to the moon and planets a slight parallax is observable, and on the analogy of terrestrial parallax astronomers are able to calculate what they call the distance of these bodies. Perhaps their calculations are right, but the magnitudes are not conceivable as associative distance, being so much greater than we have any experience of. We take them to mean that the heavenly bodies are extremely degraded, perspectively speaking. Their noumena are in contact with our minds, for this is essential to perception, but if astronomical calculations are correct the contact is infinitely slight, compared with what it would be, supposing—to speak realistically—we could go to the stars or they could be brought to us.

Berkeley's *Theory of Vision* and *Dialogues* are occupied with the analysis of perspection. The arguments he uses to show that distance outwards is not real are in the main those given in this section.

XXV—CONCRETION

IF we take a cricket-ball in the hand and turn it round we shall perceive a series of discs. Only one of these can be seen at a time, but if we perceive and remember the whole series we shall be able to infer all from the perception of one in a similar object. The same occurs with other cubical or solid objects. This is a form of ideal construction different from any we have yet considered. It differs from inherence in that the object which we conceptually put together is never objectively perceived as a whole. It is an imaginary whole constructed in the intellect out of fragmentary experience. It differs from association on the same grounds; the latter can be all perceived at once in forming the judgment. It differs from perspection in that the imperfection of experience is due to curtailment, not to general deterioration. What we actually see may be perspectively perfect. It differs also from the next category in that the series of perceptions can occur in various orders of succession.

The 'backs' of Things. We talk of the back of a thing, but nobody has ever seen a back. Things have no backs in the popular sense of the word. When we turn round a back to perceive it, it is then a front. Everything is a flat upright surface, and its appearance of solidity can be imitated on a surface known to be flat, and with nearly the same illusive completeness as in the original object. In turning things round we merely change the surface; we are exercising our power to alter primary consciousness.

When two persons perceive the 'same' object from contrary directions, the sameness means that the two objects proceed from the same cause, or can be reduced to the same general idea. But the objects are numerically distinct. By a similar turn of speech we say that A and *a* are the same *letter*, but they are evidently distinct and dissimilar objects. If we hold a thing before a mirror and see what is termed its back, we produce a new object resembling the first in some respects but without its resistance.

Resistance is a negative term signifying the limit of our power to alter primary experience. Where our power ceases resistance is said to begin, and we meet with resistance when we apply a power inadequate to the desired effect.

Dr. Johnson's solitary experiment in idealistic philosophy has been often related. He struck a post, and because it did not disappear he thought he had disproved Berkeley's statement that material objects exist only in the perceiving mind. The experiment merely showed that all means are not adequate to change all primary experience. Had he shut his eyes, or turned a corner, or occupied his attention with other matters, the post would have vanished. He chose improper means and therefore met with 'resistance.' No idealist believes we can change our primary experience by any capricious and frivolous means [1].

[1] Probably Dr Johnson meant to be humorous in his way. The principles of Idealism are apt to excite mirth in the unphilosophical, but the laugh is not always on the side of the scoffer. A member of the Persian philosophical sect called Samradians once said to his steward: 'The world and its inhabitants have no actual existence; they have merely an ideal being.' The servant on hearing this took the first favourable opportunity to conceal his master's horse, and when he was about to ride brought him an ass with the horse's saddle. When the Samradian asked, 'Where is the horse?'—the servant replied, 'Thou hast been thinking of an idea; there was no horse in being.' The master answered, 'It is true'; he then mounted the ass, and after riding for some time he suddenly dismounted and taking the saddle off the ass's back placed it on the servant's, drawing the girths tightly; and having forced the bridle into his mouth, he mounted him and flogged him along vigorously. The servant in piteous accents exclaimed, 'What is the meaning of this treatment?'—to which the Samradian replied, 'There is no such thing as a whip; it is merely ideal; thou art only thinking of some illusion.' After which the steward repented and restored the horse.

Another Samradian—or perhaps the same individual—having married the daughter of a rich man, she, on finding out her husband's creed, proposed to have some amusement at his expense. One day the Samradian brought in a bottle of pure wine, which during his absence she emptied of its contents and filled with water. When the time for taking wine arrived she poured out water instead of wine, into a gold cup which was her own property. The Samradian having observed, 'Thou hast given me water instead of wine,'—she answered, 'It is only ideal;

Geographical Concretion. The knowledge of large geographical areas is an artificial construction without objective reality.

Our experience is, literally and exactly, a series or sequence—a flux or stream. It is composed of objects or of groups, according to the width of our attention. If we travel over a large tract of country the experience is a train of objects or views, which follow each other continuously but for interruptions in attention. If we were bound to think of things in the order in which they were experienced, we should have to imagine our topographical consciousness as a long ribbon of views, like the pictures of a panorama. Supposing we travelled hither and thither over one county, it would appear to us as a straight strip of land which might be several hundred miles long. If we again traversed the ground, but in another order, we should have another strip resembling the first, but also differing from it, and it would be necessary to keep the two from being confused in our mind. If several persons traversed the same ground but in divers directions, they would each retain a different

there was no wine in existence.' The husband then said, 'Thou hast spoken well; hand me the cup that I may go to a neighbour's house and bring it back full of wine.' He thereupon took out the gold cup, which he sold, and instead of it brought back an earthen vessel full of wine. The wife on seeing this said, 'What hast thou done with the golden cup?' He replied, 'Thou art surely thinking of some ideal golden cup'—on which the woman greatly regretted her witticism.—*Dabistán*, v. i. p. 199-200.

recollection of it, and it would be extremely hard for any two of them to agree as to the order in succession of any portion of the ground traversed.

Our experience of the natural group suggests a mode of treating our geographical experience which overcomes many of these inconveniences. We find that we can traverse (either bodily or by the eye) a single landscape in a thousand directions, and retain a memory of it without any reference to these directions. What we remember is the mutual positions of the objects, not the order in which they were observed. As this greatly facilitates the memory of one group, we apply the same principle of synthesis to the succession of groups composing our geographical experience. We dismiss from our minds the order of observation, and construct instead an imaginary group of associated objects or places having mutual positions. It is imaginary, for no one has ever seen as a co-existent synthesis the objects of a county, not to speak of a country or continent. Substituting for memory of succession, a memory of position, there grows up in our mind a large coexistent image of a country on the model of a single group, which affords all the advantages as regards economy of energy which we enjoy by virtue of comprehending a natural group in one act of consciousness.

Take an instance of this economy. Suppose a man

travelled from London to Oxford, then to Exeter, then to Portsmouth, then to Brighton, and afterwards desired to return to London. If he, acting on a mistaken conception of truth and disdaining instruction from others, persisted in remembering the objects perceived on his journey as—what they no doubt literally were—a continuous series, he would be unable to imagine any way of returning to London except by reversing the order of his journey. If on the other hand he carried in his mind an image of the ground in question, with the mutual position of the places, it would enable him to *foresee* that London was to be reached by journeying northward from Brighton, in far less time and at far less cost than by returning the way he came. Thus does conceptual position, when it is correctly imagined, prove its superiority to the order of experience. And we say that the ideal picture is truer than the crude memory, —not that it is really so if natural order is a test of truth, but because it is the least onerous, which is our practical standard of truth. The only object of knowledge being the wise management of energy, that sort of knowledge must be considered truest that enables us to have the feelings we desire at the least cost. In one sense truth means the quickest and easiest way of passing from one state of consciousness to another preconceived state.

It may be objected to the above example as a valid

deduction from an imaginary synthesis, that the relation of London to Brighton is now a certainty, whereas an inference can be no more than a probability. The reply is, that if a man has already traversed the route in question, it is to him an actual experience and his idea of it is ever afterwards a memory, not an inference. But until it is actually perceived it must be imaginary, and therefore slightly problematical. Although a man is convinced that others are not deceiving him in saying a place is to be reached in a certain way, he cannot be absolutely sure that he fully understands the directions given, in other words, that his image of the route corresponds to their perception of it. There probably never is exact similarity between one man's primary experience and another man's idea of it. It may even be doubted whether there is ever exact similarity between a man's own primary experience and his subsequent idea of it.

The geographical synthesis is founded on actual exploration supplemented by inference. The mutual position of some important places are determined and serve as precedents for a multitude of minor positional deductions. A is twenty miles north of London, B is ten miles south of London, hence A is thirty miles north of B. The mileage is determined by imagining the synthesis developed into natural groups and measured laterally. Other scales are the time spent in travelling between the places, or the money it costs, or the distance delineated on a map.

Though the geographical concretion may be modelled on the association, we cannot treat it perspectively, for the places being purely ideal (except the one we are at), the ideal image is not liable to deterioration by weakened perception. It may suffer degradation by forgetfulness, but that has nothing to do with perspection.

Sphericity of the Earth. The geographical synthesis is not always formed on the pattern of a natural association. That is the first and most obvious shape to give it, and for thousands of years it appears to have answered the topographical needs of mankind. But as exploration extended it was found that the associative theory did not in some cases afford true preconception. If we travel far enough in any fixed direction we shall return to the point from which we started. This could not have been predicted from a synthesis formed on the model of a landscape. Such a return however takes place in the objects denominated spheres, and so the spherical instead of the flat form has been conceptually given to the geographical concretion. That is all that is meant by saying that the world is round. There is no world, as the mystical realist—projecting outwards his mental synthesis—imagines. There is only a scheme of spherical positions in the intellect, which facilitates the recollection of places and enables us to foresee the shortest and easiest way of reaching—*i.e.* experiencing places. The concretion is true inasmuch as the prediction is found to coincide with real experience. But that by no means implies that the places exist except when perceived in minds.

XXVI—SEQUENCE

SEQUENCE is a series most resembling a procession of objects in a natural group (second category). It differs therefrom in that the objects cannot be seen together. It differs from concretion in that the order in which the objects appear cannot be altered, or if they are human and alterable we cease to treat them as a sequence. They no longer have the predictive value which moves us to form artificial groups of objects.

Satisfactory examples of reasoning in sequence are less numerous than might be supposed. It is a poor category for argument. Series either occur with perfect regularity, like the seasons of the year, phases of the moon, &c., and then they rapidly become mere recollections and lose the problematical character essential to a true inference, or the connection between the objects is too casual for argumentative purposes. Darwin's theory of the formation of coral atolls is a fine argument in sequence, but the application of this theory to reefs not examined by him is hardly uncertain enough to be an argument. It is the first sequential inference that is valid—the rest are foregone conclusions.

Geology supplies some good sequences. It has been noticed, for instance, that the sea leaves ripple-marks on sandy beaches, and stones with similar marks have been found at a distance from the sea; it is a valid sequential inference that the marks in the latter case have also been formed by the action of the waves. Here the difference in locality between the two compared series—the modern complete and the ancient incomplete—supplies that slight element of doubt essential to an argument.

So as regards the mode of making ancient flint tools: it has been found that tools exactly similar to the ancient can now be made with the simplest possible means, and it is a true argument to infer that the ancient implements were made by these means. The conclusion is highly probable without being infallibly certain, and that is what a dialectical conclusion ought to be.

We may admit that some of the astronomical sequences are forms of reasoning, for they were such to their first discoverers, and to minds not thoroughly conversant with them they are still in the nature of predictions that might fail of accomplishment. Political, financial, and sporting forecasts are sequential arguments, and we may also include speculations on the future states of all growing organisms and developing institutions.

Time. The intervals between the objects of a sequence are imagined after the model of lateral intervals in association. This is Time. Like space it is mere blanks in experience, though treated by realists as external and self-subsisting. It can be measured by reference to objects on whose sequential recurrence we have the most reliance, such as the phases of the moon, the positions of the sun in the ecliptic, the movements of the hands of a clock or the chiming of its bells. Abstract or unbounded time is called 'eternity'; like abstract space it is a refined form of nothing. Time and space are usually coupled together as if co-ordinate, but eternity is the co-ordinate of space. Time is divided sequence and would correspond to materially divided space, that is, space with objects in it at regular intervals.

Matter, space, and time are the three pillars of the realistic world. We have now seen what they are made of. Matter is a general idea compiled by ourselves from phenomenal consciousness. It is no substance—only an average. Space has even less reality. It is first the interval between two objects in association; then this interval is used metaphorically as an expression and measure of perspective decadence. Time is an application of the same associative interval to express the blanks between objects in sequence. Space and time are thus pure nullities—negatives with positive names. These three notions being exploded as entities, there remain as a residuum of true fact and the starting-point of philosophy—*minds*, their *energies*, and their *consciousness*. This is a very ancient triad.

Science constantly confounds sequence and causation. We are told that the moon *causes* eclipses of the sun, that heat *causes* objects to expand, that a seal *causes* an imprint. This is a metaphor from human causation, and the expression is now so rooted in language that it would hardly be possible to introduce a more correct phraseology. Yet it is as incorrect as to say that one o'clock causes two o'clock, or that daylight causes darkness. The confusion has arisen from the fact that both sequence and causation deal with fixed inconvertible series, but only in the latter is there real power exerted to produce the effect. Material things and their apparent effects are due to a cause lying behind both.

XXVII—CAUSATION

CAUSATION differs from all other categories in that one of its elements is mental. It is a series beginning in the mind—in this relation denominated *cause*—and developing into objective phenomena called *effects* or an effect. The series being known by judgment we can infer similar causes from perception of similar effects. The commonest causation is the use and interpretation of language. Because we utter words from a certain motive we infer that all who utter the same words do so from the same motive. That is the reason of the intelligibility of words.

This category is peculiar from the extremely narrow range of the experience which supplies the judgments. We never perceive any mind but one—our own—and this has to supply all the judgments by which we reason concerning other minds. There is therefore no category in which correct reasoning is so difficult and so rare. No amount of experience entirely overcomes this defect, for if we are ignorant we cannot understand the wise, and if we are wise we cannot conceive the motives of the ignorant and vicious.

Only those persons who are mentally very like each other are mutually comprehensible.

This category has a further peculiarity. In all the rest the inference relates to objective experience, and this being due to interaction of minds we are justified in saying that until it is perceived it has no existence. But in causation we are inferring something with reference to a mind, and this exists though we never can perceive it. We know that minds exist without perception because we know that our own exists though no one perceives us—though we are in total darkness and silence and cannot ourselves perceive our bodies. As already stated, Existence has not the same meaning when applied to objects and to minds, objects being merely temporary conditions of minds. The non-existence of inferred but unperceived objects does not follow from any defect in the faculty of inference, but depends on the essential character of objects. They are created by mutual contact of minds and cannot exist without that condition, however clearly they may be inferred and however correctly their appearance may be predicted.

Causation is confounded with sequence because both are series. Let me illustrate the difference between them by an example. I turn the stop-cock of a pipe, and water flows from the open end of the pipe. In popular and even scientific language it would be said that I caused the water to flow. But this is incorrect. All I caused was the turning of the tap; that alone was wholly due to my energy and intelligence. There followed as a sequence the outflow of water, but that was due partly to cosmic force and partly to the previous human causation (not mine) implied in making and laying down the pipe so as to utilise the cosmic force. I merely removed an obstacle that prevented the further development of the force in a particular direction. My relation to the outflow was sequence, not causation.

In observation sequence registers fixed or probable series of *objects* without regard to their causes. It is sufficient if they occur regularly enough to justify prediction. Causation, on the other hand, pays no regard to physical connection of any sort, but seeks out the being or beings who supplied the energy producing an effect or series of effects. The speculations in causation pass quite beyond the domain of objectivity, over into the realm of true creation.

When we read that 'the succession of events is an endless chain of effects which are in their turn causes of new effects,' what is meant is sequence, and for 'cause' and 'effect' the terms 'antecedent' and 'consequent' should have been employed. Sequences may be 'chains' and may be long, but if so their links have been forged by independent causes acting *across* the chain; as when a line of soldiers fire in succession at regular intervals, or as in the case of the moon's quarters. In these instances the objects, although forming a series, has each a cause of its own.

Certainly a causation is a series, for the cause precedes the effect. But an effect is never the cause of a succeeding effect. When this appears to be the case the explanation is that the energy was not exhausted in producing the immediate simple effect, but has produced a complicated effect in which a series may be discovered. An objective effect, being a mere flash of consciousness—a shadow on a window-blind—is incapable of causing anything.

Analysis of Cause. Cause is mind in action. It consists of at least energy and a sentimental *motive*—energy exerted to gratify sentiment. If the mind is intellectualised there will probably be an ideal element in the cause—in this connection called *plan* or *design*—for the better direction of the energy. Normal human causation consists of an effort of mind directed towards the objective realisation of a plan, for the gratification of a sentiment. This is the same as WILL.

All three elements of cause may be furnished by the same individual—or any two of them—or only one. For instance, the man who wants a house supplies the motive, the architect provides the design, the builder finds the energy.

One plan may use up an indefinite number of separate stores of energy. Even in an individual the realisation of a plan exhausts the powers of millions of organic cells. A military campaign illustrates the relation of plan to power. The design may have been formed by one man, and then communicated wholly or partially to a hundred thousand, and the energies of these may be devoted to its realisation. The soldier fights with his own energy, but he is directed by his commander's idea, or so much of it as has been confided to him. The design may stretch from the commander to the soldier, but not the energy. In order that the commander should be termed the 'cause' of his private's activity, it would be necessary to eliminate the notion of exerted energy from causation, and reduce it to bare communication of design, which would be absurd.

The stretching of one design over many relays of energy has no doubt helped to confirm the notion that causation is a long chain of alternate causes and effects. The truth is that energy can act only at short range, and has to be incessantly renewed. The world is in a constant state of creation and dissolution, say the Kabbalists. It is absurd to speak of anything that existed a thousand or even a hundred years ago as the *cause* of anything existing to-day. The design may intellectually survive, but the energy is long since dissipated. We have never more than about a day's supply of energy in store at once.

If sentiment, power, and design are supplied by different individuals, no single one of them can be called the cause of the effect. The relation of each to the result is sequence. When we have traced an effect to the mind or minds that supplied the three or the two necessary elements—supposing the design is sometimes omitted and the act what we call *instinctive* —we have obtained a complete explanation of the effect. Our curiosity is then absolutely satisfied. We have reached a true beginning.

It is the want of this thorough explanation that renders material science so disappointing. We are put off with a mere physical antecedent, which itself needs explanation as much as its consequent. It does not make the antecedent more significant to place it far back in time, for time by itself is not a cause—it is merely a name given to intervals of experience. A thing is never truly explained until we see that its production either caused pleasure to something else, or was expected to cause pleasure. Behind everything must be Sentiment.

One generation of beings is not the cause of the following generation, else the former would have perished in begetting the latter. More particularly, a man is not the *effect* of his parents or remoter ancestors, though they stood to him in an antecedent relation. The seed of his body was taken from theirs, but his energy is his own, drawn direct from the universal source. If he resembles them corporeally it is because he previously resembled them mentally, not because the cells of his body have hereditary tendencies to take particular forms. Hence the Darwinian genealogy of men and animals—supposing it were correct—does not explain them. It is a phenomenal schematism based on or implying an erroneous assumption—that generation is causation.

Atomism—the theory of Democritus—is founded on another false view of causation. The physical parts of a thing are conceived to be the causes of the thing, and so the least conceivable particles of 'matter' are considered the first causes and true explanation of all things. This notion appears to be useful in chemistry, but it cannot be accepted as philosophy. If our senses were sharpened to perceive atoms these would simply be small phenomena, and it would still be necessary to inquire what motive and power produced them. It has been suggested that atoms may be inherently sentient and dynamic: if so they are minute animals or cells, and we are still without an explanation of their occurrence in organised masses. It is inconceivable that they should spontaneously enter into intricate combinations, whose evident purpose has only an indirect and partial bearing on their welfare.

Though advocated by men of undoubted ability, Atomism and Evolution are nothing more than forms of the ordinary realistic belief, that things are caused by their physical antecedents. The two theories are supposed to be complementary, but in reality they are contradictory. If an animal body is caused by its parents it cannot be caused by its own atoms, and *vice versâ*.

Varieties of Causation. Abstract causation—the category—consists of a cause and an effect. The former, as we have seen, is complicated, the latter may comprise several objects. Ignoring the complications involved in the use of an organism—which comes between the mind and the final effect—we distinguish four or five varieties of causation.

$$C - e^1 - e^2 - e^3 - e^4$$

The cause C produces from its own energy the series of effects $e^1 - e^4$, like the rebounding of a missile from the surface of ground or water. This may be called 'ricochet.'

Effects, each having an independent cause, sometimes form a series like a ladder:

$$\begin{array}{ccccc} e^1 & e^2 & e^3 & e^4 & e^5 \\ | & | & | & | & | \\ C & C & C & C & C \end{array}$$

This is the species illustrated by a successive discharge of musketry. The causation of science consists of the *effects* in this species considered apart from the causes.

In the 'gamut' the effects are in sequence, but they have all the same physical antecedent.

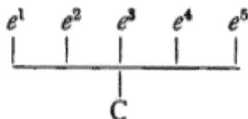

The successive acts of the same man or animal are of this kind.

In each of these species the effects are in series and may be treated as a sequence, but the cause or causes lie outside the sequence. Far from mere regularity of succession being a proof of causation between the objects, it may very easily be itself a part of the causal design.

In the 'capstan' several partial causes contribute to produce one effect, as when a gang of men manipulate one engine.

The 'star' or 'fountain' is the converse of the last.

A single cause produces several simultaneous partial

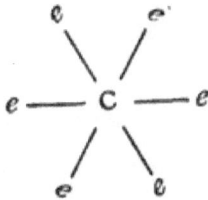

effects, as when we strike our open hand smartly on the surface of water.

These sub-categories enable us, if we so wish, to define an energic series somewhat more precisely than by calling it a causation in the most abstract sense. Possibly also the figures delineated represent the primitive forms which energy takes when emerging into the phenomenal. The 'star' is a most characteristic form. The dendritic shape so frequently met with in objects is a star springing from a ray of a preceding star. Perhaps each vegetable bud has an independent cause; if not they are 'ricochets' from the general plant life. In the combinations of these elementary effects we have a likely explanation of plant and crystal formation.

'Conservation' of Energy. Energy is annihilated in the using. It emanates from a great universal centre, and at a short distance from that centre is completely and irrecoverably dissipated. The apparent fixity of things is purely formal—like the fixity

of a water-fall, which renews its substance every few seconds. That is the meaning of saying that the world is in a constant state of formation and dissolution.

Physical theorists represent energy under the figure of substance, but they suppose it is fixed in *quantity* though constantly undergoing change of *form*—the scientific view, here as elsewhere, being just the opposite of the philosophical.

Observe—say the conservationists—the case of a man raising a heavy stone from the earth. He fatigues himself but he does not destroy energy; he acquires command over the energy-in-position of the stone, and in using it to crack a cocoa-nut or drive a post he receives back his own energy undiminished in quantity.

That seems reasonable at first sight. A quantity of energy is taken from the man and put into the stone; it is taken from the stone and put into the driven post. To be sure, if the man undrives the post he does not thereby disfatigue himself, as the theory would lead us to expect—he fatigues himself the more.

The same 'law,' we are told, holds good in building a dam across a stream and utilising the force of water to drive a mill. The energy apparently lost in the construction is recovered in the superior ease with which we grind our corn or saw our timber. There is a confusion in the terminology here: to save energy that would otherwise be lost is not identical with recovering energy that has once been used.

We make a gun, load it, and discharge a bullet against a target. What has become of the force expended? It has been transformed into heat, say the conservationists. And when the target and flattened bullet have cooled down? The energy has gone to raise the general temperature of the universe!

That is a conclusion hard to believe and impossible to verify. But—granting that the individual explosions of a gun may be the 'conservation' of some antecedent power—how do we recover the initial expense of the instrument? And if not recoverable, where at least and in what form does it exist? Prior to the explosions that are represented by heated targets and the like, energy was spent in inventing and making the gun, making the ammunition, loading and aiming the piece. All these were essential to the effect—and what has become of them? Have they also gone to warm the universe?

Instead of raising a stone to a height, let us carry it along horizontally till we feel the same degree of fatigue. If energy in the using is merely transformed but not lost, we should now be in possession of some power equivalent to the energy expended. But we are not—we have nothing to show for our trouble.

If we construct a water-mill and fix it high and dry in the middle of a plain, instead of under a fall of water, we get no return for the energy expended. By such a law as the conservation of energy, and with the usefulness of a properly placed mill as the measure of compensation, we should receive an equivalent return no matter where the mill is placed. What has *place* to do with the action of a universal law?

Instead of raising the stone or carrying it horizontally, let us find it near the edge of a precipice and roll it over. There is no proportion between the push that launched the stone, and the force it exhibits on reaching the foot of the precipice. How is the equivalence of energy maintained in this case? It will be replied that the force now at work is gravitation. If so, it was gravitation that brought down the first stone on the post—not any energy transferred from us to the stone. The raising of the stone put us in a position to use the force of gravity, just as climbing the precipice put us in a position to roll the stone over the edge of it.

Such considerations as these make this 'law' incredible to me. But when I pass from the explanation to the concrete facts, I have no difficulty in

understanding them. It is the law that is obscure—
not the facts.

There exists nothing but living minds of different
degrees of energy. We men are small beings associated with a cosmical creature whose force is im-
measurably greater than ours, and we have intelligence
enough to utilise part of this force to supplement our
own. That is the meaning of *mechanism*. Some
efforts to control the cosmic forces are profitable, but
there is no transmutation of our energy into the
result, nor any necessary equivalence between the
labour and the result. We may stumble upon an
available cosmic force almost by accident—we may
waste a life-time over a mechanical problem and fail
to solve it.

The utilisation of cosmic force by man is best explained by comparing it with animal slavery. Trap
a wild elephant and train him to draw and carry—
you have constructed an engine. There are of course
important differences between the two kinds of instrument, due to the enormous disproportion between
the magnitude and power of the respective entities.
In the case of the animal the whole life comes under
our control: in the case of the cosmos we can utilise
only a minute fraction of it, and that rather by
putting ourselves in its way than by making it obey
us. The animal we have to feed: the cosmic being
does not draw upon us for its nourishment. We

can direct the animal through his sensibility: the cosmic sensibility appears to be beyond our power of irritation.

Apart from these differences the general laws of the one kind of tool are those of the other also. We have not transferred power to the raised stone, or the coiled spring, or the loaded gun, or the embanked river—any more than to the tamed and harnessed horse. There is no fixed ratio between the fatigue of catching and training an animal, and the energy saved by making him work for us. The animal's work is not our own energy given back to us—neither is the machine's. A plough is useless without cattle to draw it—so is a turbine without water to drive it. When coal is burned to 'generate' electricity, that is the cosmic equivalent of exhausting or killing one animal to overpower or to feed another: the energy of combustion is utterly destroyed—not transformed into the electricity.

The question can be more accurately stated and brought to a plain issue if we use the terms and forms of dialectic.

A theory is an argument—when it is not a fallacy—and an argument, we have seen, consists of two parts. There is the matter of fact requiring explanation, and the antecedent knowledge which is used to illustrate it. Of these the precedent is the more important, and it is no valid objection to a criticism that the person who offers it knows less about the *case* than the theorist. The critic may be in possession of a better precedent, which the theorist has failed to notice, perhaps from a too exclusive attention to the case.

In the question before us the case is Mechanical or Inorganic Energy. It is not an object, but an inference from the knowledge of our personal mental energy. This latter is the only energy we really perceive. But we find in objects, or associated with the perception of them, a power capable of assisting or of opposing our efforts—hence we conclude it is something of the same nature as our own power. We cannot well avoid that inference, and there is no apparent reason why we should try to avoid it.

So far science and philosophy are at one, but here they part company. Philosophy consistently endows Nature with sentiency also, for we never—to our certain knowledge—meet with energy without sentiency, and we have no right to transfer one attribute without the other.

Although science is indebted to the assimilation of organic and inorganic—Nature explained by Man—for the first notion of external energy, no sooner is the notion formed than the argument is discarded, and external energy is declared to be entirely destitute of an organic and mental character. How then is it to be further explained? To what shall it now be likened?

In the materialistic scheme all things are supposed to be resolved into matter and force. Matter is conceived as a self-existent substance, indestructible, &c. It is better known than force, for material things can be directly perceived whereas force is imaginary all the time. Under these circumstances it is natural though illogical to treat force as a species of matter. With only two things left in the universe, the better known of the two will be used to explain the less known, if an explanation is considered indispensable. Force is accordingly brought as a 'case' under matter as a 'precedent,' and is concluded to be indestructible because matter is believed to be indestructible; and when energy appears to be wasted the inference is that it has simply withdrawn from view, like an object that has ceased to be perceived and may be perceived again. That seems to be the evolution of the scientific notion of inorganic energy.

This theorem is fallacious in two respects. There is no such matter as science imagines. Matter is a general idea formed by the study of material objects, which are states of consciousness excited by noumenal contact. It is the average object—a mere affection or formation of the observing mind. *We* are the makers of matter. Such an idea cannot be said to be indestructible: in a sense it is destroyed in an individual when it is forgotten or inactive; it would certainly be destroyed if all minds ceased to form it. Thus the precedent in the scientific theory of force is itself false.

Then energy is not in the least like matter—either the matter of science or that of philosophy. The energy we really know is a unique experience—not a general idea, nor anything analogous to a phenomenal object; so that even if the proposed precedent were true in itself, it is not applicable to the case. To complete our knowledge of external energy we must go back to that comparison which first suggested to us that there is external energy, namely, the comparison of living man with living nature.

If this is not a correct account of the derivation of the notion that cosmic energy is indestructible, let conservationists tell us what is the parallel on which they are arguing. Here is a blank theorem for completion—

x	is indestructible
Cosmic energy is a sort of x	*it must therefore be considered indestructible*

Matter, as we have seen, is not x. Human energy is not x. Our individual power—so far as experience informs us—is destroyed in the using. A day's work exhausts us, and we have to pass into the condition called sleep to be refilled. It is sleep, not food, that refreshes the mind. Food restores the bodily tool we have been working with—puts a fresh edge on the chisel,—but it does not recuperate the power that wields the tool.

What then is x?

NOTE ON DREAMS

If dreams could be studied with our waking consciousness they would throw much light on our mental nature. Being a poor dreamer myself I am not competent to discuss this phase of psychology as it deserves. I think however the bulk of our dreams can be reduced to two principles. There is first the simple lowering of the mental energy, which weakens the attention and dissolves the artificial categories, thus making ordinary reason impossible. There is just enough energy left to revive a few scattered ideas, which blend together without control or regard to precedent. Hence the singular combinations they sometimes form.

In the waking state the objective and intellectual experience are generally more vivid and engrossing than the sentimental—at least in masculine persons. (I deliberately avoid the phrase 'masculine mind,' because there is manifestly no sex in mind.) In dreams the converse of this is the case. The objects we appear to see are dull and indistinct, being ideas mistaken for objects, whilst the feelings are evidently genuine and sometimes of great intensity. This may be explained on the occult principle alluded to in section x.

What I understand by occult influence is this. In ordinary experience the object is first perceived, then a sentiment may be excited either by the same noumenon or by recollection. In the occult procedure this order is reversed. The sentiment is first secretly reached through the chinks of our intellectual armour, and the intellect is not excited at all or only by association. During sleep, when the Self is nearly exhausted of power, it is likely we are more exposed than usual to such influences. They invade our mind and excite our sentiment without awaking the intellect. Whatever ideas accompany the sentiments are generally inadequate to explain them, the stock of available ideas being now reduced.

The conversations we hold in dreams, and the apparent communication of knowledge that takes place, are referred by Du Prel to a division of the ego into two or more individuals who talk together. This notion appears to me forced and unthinkable. Under what image is the ego figured that it should be capable of division? In the waking state we sometimes ask ourselves questions, and on consideration find answers to them. We cannot recall a name, a word, or date, though we know it is somewhere in our memory, and we pause and search till we succeed in exciting the latent image. When this takes place in a dream the information is assumed to come from another individual by an easy dramatisation.

A disturbance in the body during sleep may constitute—like all bodily suffering—a drain upon our mental energy, which will be felt as a sentiment and may excite ideas by sympathy. No doubt many dreams are caused in this manner.

Since our waking consciousness is highly artificial and imaginary, we may infer that whilst dreaming we are nearer to the natural, primitive state of the mind, but in a weakened condition.

REDACTION OF COLLOQUIAL ARGUMENTS

XXVIII

A CLEVER man has said that the use of language is to conceal thought. Its primary use is certainly not to reveal thought, but to enable one person to produce an effect on the mind of another or of others, either for their or his own advantage. In the course of using speech as an instrument of command, entreaty, persuasion, menace, or fustigation, it may happen that the movements of the speaker's mind are revealed to some extent, but this is a mere incident, not the main purpose of the speech.

Grammar is the system of rules which govern the use of language in its primary and ordinary capacity.

It follows from this that language is in no sense a revelation of the reasoning processes, nor do the rules of grammar coincide with the laws of intellect. It is just as reasonable to expect to find the metaphysic of thought revealed in any of the industrial and fine arts, as to look for it in the structure of speech. Aristotle drew his logic from the composition of the Greek sentence—he might as well have sought for logic in the constitution of the Greek buskin.[1]

Even when men begin to reason aloud and seek to render their logical movements as evident as possible, they are so hampered by the ordinary habits and rules of speech that their meaning is often difficult or impossible of comprehension. Whence arises the necessity, if we would reason aloud to any purpose, of redacting or translating language from the vernacular into a dialect more indicative of the logical processes that take place when we reason.

This redaction consists mainly in distinguishing clearly the four parts composing an argument, namely, the Subject of the Precedent; the Case which is brought under it for judgment; the Applicate or part of the precedent bearing on the case; the Conclusion, which is the ideal judgment concerning

[1] Though evidently suggested by language, the form which the syllogistic logic finally assumed is so unlike anything grammatical, that it is easily convertible into symbols having no resemblance to language. It has been put into literal symbols with algebraic values, and into geometrical diagrams. A logical machine has even been invented by Professor Jevons, 'worked by keys like a pianoforte,' which returns 'infallible answers'—of the Aristotelian sort—to every kind of question. That is sufficiently unlike both reason and language.

the case. When these four parts are expressed and clearly understood we have a perfect argument, so far as argumentation depends on language. But probably we have spoiled the language from the grammatical and rhetorical point of view. We may have had to supply much that would be redundant and unsightly in ordinary conversation or writing, and to take away much that is appropriate to colloquial discourse. We are diverting language to a use for which it was not designed, and we need not be surprised if the result is ungraceful. This cannot be helped since there exists no other means than language by which to express our concrete reasoning.

I have already shown practically how an argument can be arranged so as to indicate the logical relations subsisting between its parts. A Greek cross is drawn, and in the four angles thus made the four parts of the argument are written, or the principal words of each. Begin with the conclusion, for that is generally the most explicitly given; then find or supply the part of the precedent that agrees or logically rhymes with it; next place the subject in the first compartment, and the case under it. These relative positions should not be varied. When this has been practiced for a while it enables one to dismember the most intricate argument with ease and exactness.

The redaction or re-writing of the language can be abbreviated by regarding the horizontal line as equivalent to a declaration of resemblance between case and precedent-subject, and (by application) between the illustrative abstraction and conclusion. If there is an argument at all there must be this resemblance, and the right-hand parts must have one of the six categorical relations to the left-hand parts. The contents of the angles may be cut down to a word or two, as—

I.

Tyrants	death
Caesar	*death*

If the category be further indicated by a numeral over the upright line, we have the essential parts of the argument in a very compact form. The cross and categorical numeral may be regarded as a sufficient substitute for grammatical syntax and punctuation.

The negative word that generally occurs in stigmatic arguments requires special attention. It should always be put in the second angle, and when it may read so as to negative the subject it should be hyphened to the predicate, thus giving it the value of *non, un, im,* or other negative prefix. To say colloquially that 'all Russians are not angels' leaves room to believe that some Russians are angels, the 'not' applying to 'all' instead of to 'angels.' By linking 'not' to 'angels' we get a term equivalent to non-angelic, which expresses the meaning intended—that no Russians are angels.

Caution should be observed with partitive words like 'some,' 'many,' 'a few,' &c. There is little danger of ambiguity when they occur in the case, for that means that we bring only a portion of a group of things to judgment, which we are manifestly entitled to do. The conclusion however applies only to the portion in question, not to the rest of the group. 'Honest men deserve respect; some Negroes are honest men; *these particular Negroes deserve respect.*'

In the precedent, partitive words imply that only some of the subject have the applicate. If that portion is a dialectical 'all'—that is, if there has been no exception in the course of our experience—we may, though that experience has been limited, venture to treat the applicate as universal and ground a conclusion upon it. If the subject is really partitive—if we know for certain that some subjects have the applicate and others have it not—the conclusion must follow the greater probability. If the number and character of the observed cases is known we can express the probability arithmetically; it is the number of occurrences of a given character divided by the total number.

Redaction must not be used to correct original errors of observation; its purpose is to render explicit in language what is implicit in thought, not what might have been thought supposing the thinker had been more intelligent or industrious than he was.

'Conversion' is a process admitted or required in the artificial methods of syllogistic dialectic. It consists mainly in transposing the subject and predicate of a proposition, as 'some Europeans are Mohammedans'—'some Mohammedans are Europeans.' This operation never takes place in real argument, or is merely the emendation of a proposition at first awkwardly expressed. Conversion can take place only when the predicate is a class, hence the categorical propositions cannot be converted.

FALLACIES

XXIX—OF EQUIVOCATION AND MAL-OBSERVATION

FALLACIES are counterfeit or sham arguments. They may fail to be arguments—(1) because their antecedents are false ; (2) because the antecedents though true are not arranged dialectically, and do not suggest the right conclusion ; (3) because the language is equivocal.

To take the last first. So many things are called by the same name, and so many different names may be applied to the same thing, that if we attempt to argue from words alone, without any personal knowledge of the things or judgments that are in question, we shall certainly make mistakes. The only security against this sort of fallacy is much experience, and the self-denial necessary to relinquish argument and the criticism of arguments, when we have no sufficient knowledge of the data.

The degree of imperfection in observation which should be considered to render the theorem fallacious, is no easy matter to determine. One class of logicians (the Formal) get over the difficulty by declaring that dialectic is not concerned with concrete knowledge at all,[1] but only with its general properties (as conceived by Aristotle), and they have set up as a standard of logical truth the capability of being imagined. A centaur is to them as true a fact as a horse, and they would accept as valid such a theorem as this: 'All centaurs object to be shod with iron; Gryneus is a centaur; therefore we may conclude that he would resist being shod with iron.' No amount of conceivability or formal coherence can make this other than nonsense.

J. S. Mill and his followers go to the opposite extreme. They study all the sciences and endeavour to master their methods of reasoning—which is well; but they do so with the prepossession that there exists some absolute standard of knowledge to fail in attaining which involves fallacy. They thus condemn as false all theorems based on superseded notions of nature and man. Only modern thinkers can argue rationally—the ancients were all and habitu-

---

[1] One fault of observation is noticed by formal logicians; it is that of assigning an improper cause, *Non causa pro causâ* or *Post hoc ergo propter hoc*. It is evident that defects in every other category have an equal right to be noticed.

ally victims of fallacy,—and of the moderns only the few are rational who have mastered the latest theories on every subject. This is the principle of Mill's doctrine on the fallacies of observation; we can see that he regarded all beliefs as fallacious which he had himself outgrown or did not feel a need of. 'Truth' was simply the facts and judgments that happened to suit Mill's mental constitution.

From the Substantial point of view this is an untenable position.

No degree of observation is intrinsically defective if it serve the purpose of intellect, which is to protect the mind. There is no intellectual truth as a thing in itself. The thoughts of a sparrow or a child are as perfect as those of a man, if they afford the necessary defence to the individual's sentiment. As we change our inner mental character, new intellectual ideas have to be acquired and the old are discarded, perhaps completely forgotten. They appear now to be ignorances and fallacies— mal-observation and bad reasoning. The new seem to be so much truer— perhaps infallibly true. All that is illusion. We make another advance, and the thoughts that a week before were as stable as rocks are now cast aside as absurd. Perhaps the belief in the certainty of present judgments is a condition of our making the best use of them; if so they should not be shaken until we are ready to enter on the next stage of knowledge.

It is quite true that one man may know more than another, but the ground on which the more intellectual is generally considered to be superior to the latter is not the right one. He is not better for his intellectual acquirements, but he is better if his mind, being of a finer sort, required a superior intellect to defend it. At bottom, then, the general cause of mal-observation—there are particular causes which interfere with the general rule—is inferiority of sentimental character. We do not see what we do not need to see, and we see imperfectly what is not essential to our well-being. That we should be ignorant or reason badly about what does not concern us is not in itself a defect.

It is inconsistent with these views on the function of intellect to admit that any sort of non-observation or mal-observation can be always and for all alike fallacious. If there are things which we habitually ignore, the presumption is that they do not concern us—that the knowledge they would confer is not essential to our welfare and would be intellectual lumber.

I should therefore abstain from condemning as fallacies theorems drawn in good faith from facts believed to be true, and which serve as motives of conduct. They are sophisms only when the reasoners have not taken ordinary pains to verify their data, or, knowing the antecedents to be false, pretend to believe them for some immoral purpose.

XXX—OF PARALLEL ARRANGEMENT

THERE is no fault of perversion, mutilation, or entanglement in the statement of an argument that we do not meet with in actual reasoning. Even in the writings of educated and honest thinkers it is rare to meet with an argument the parts of which are clearly distinguished by the author himself, and expressed so as to show the precise degree of force they ought to carry. Reasoning is still only a semi-conscious process directed by rule-of-thumb. We make certain statements and find they have a power of moving others, so we continue to make them. But whether the result is due to the rationality of the discourse or merely to the docility of the hearers, we do not know, and—so long as the desired result follows—we do not care to inquire.

For this state of things logicians are to a great extent responsible. They are uncritical imitators of the Greek philosophers, whose notions on dialectic were quite wrong. The Greeks and their medieval and modern followers have squandered attention on a mental process which is not reason, mistaking it for reason, so that practically there has never been a science of dialectic. However much reasoners may have wished to present their thoughts coherently, they have not been provided with a method or notation adapted to the purpose. With an instinctive sense of the futility of the Syllogism, they have ignored it completely. I cannot call to mind a single controversial work that has been presented in syllogistic form, nor do even trained logicians use it overtly in argument.[1] Yet if it were what it professes to be, it would be as natural and convenient to express our arguments in syllogism as it is to put down on paper a sum in arithmetic. We are, as regards

---

[1] Whately complains of the disinclination shown by logicians to put their rules into practice. 'Whenever they have to treat of anything that is beyond the mere elements of Logic, they totally lay aside all reference to the principles they have been occupied in establishing and explaining, and have recourse to a loose, vague, and popular kind of language; such as would be best suited indeed to an exoterical discourse but seems strangely incongruous in a professed logical treatise. . . . Surely it affords but too much plausibility to the cavils of those who scoff at Logic altogether, that the very writers who profess to teach it should never themselves make any application of, or reference to, its principles, when, and *when only*, such application and reference are to be expected.' *Logic*, Book III. Introd. The fact here admitted proves that even logicians do not find their method of any practical use. But what is the meaning of the emphatic 'when only'? Why should a logical method be unsuitable for every sort of subject except those matters of logic that are beyond the mere elements?

the expression of reasoning, in the position of numerical thinkers before the invention of figures and the elaboration of arithmetical rules. We have to do all our arguments 'in our head,' and so we do them badly. We can seldom be sure of the correctness of our own reasonings, and we are constantly being misled by sophistry. Nothing indeed will enable us to reason well or to detect false reasoning on a subject of which we are entirely ignorant, but a large measure of protection would be afforded by the adoption of a uniform system of presenting arguments, by which all the assumptions they involve are rendered explicit.

One of the commonest omissions in argumentation is to take the precedent for granted. This is allowable when it is a fact universally known or believed. 'If you let the glass fall it will be broken,'—the omitted precedent is the known consequences of letting brittle things fall to the ground. 'Caius is a liar, therefore he is a coward'—presupposes that every liar is a coward.

This liberty of suppression is sometimes used sophistically. The tacit precedent is not universally known or accepted, but if it is questioned the sophist is ready with an exclamation of surprise or contempt at our supposed ignorance. Persons who are afraid of appearing singular in their beliefs are liable to be deceived by this trick.

'It frequently happens,' says Whately, 'in the case

of a fallacy [of omitted precedent] that the hearers are left to the alternative of supplying either a premiss which is not true, or else one which does not prove the conclusion: *e.g.* if a man expatiates on the distress of the country, and thence argues that the government is tyrannical, we must suppose him to assume either that "every distressed country is under a tyranny," which is a manifest falsehood, or merely that "every country under a tyranny is distressed," which, however true, proves nothing, the Middle Term being undistributed.... Which are we to suppose the speaker meant us to understand? Surely just whichever each of his hearers might happen to prefer: some might assent to the false premiss; others allow the unsound syllogism; to the sophist himself it is indifferent, as long as they can be brought to admit the conclusion.'

We sometimes attempt to reason from *Contrast* instead of resemblance, with a confused notion that things which differ in some respects must differ also in others. 'Who spareth the rod hateth the child; the parent who loveth his child must *therefore* spare not the rod.' The fallacy of this becomes apparent when we complete the theorem in the parallel form.

VI.

The hating parent	spares the rod
The loving parent differs from the hating parent	[*No Conclusion*]

The following has often been presented as a valid argument—'What is universally believed must be true; the belief in God's existence is not universal; it is therefore not true.'

I.

What is universally believed	is true
The existence of God is not universally believed	N. C.

To establish the conclusion aimed at, it would be necessary to lay down as precedent—'What is not universally believed is not true.'

These theorems from contrast are on a par with the following—

I.

Cows	are four-footed
Sheep are not cows	*sheep are not four-footed*

This is the fallacy called in the quaint language of the syllogists 'Illicit Process of the Major Term.'

In *False Analogy* the resemblance is so slight that the application is untrustworthy, or a conclusion is drawn in excess of the resemblance. If from the habit of calling a deep bay or salt-water loch an 'arm' of the sea from its analogy to a human arm, we conclude that the sea has elbows and wrists, we commit this fallacy. The earth is like an orange, but we must not think that it is pulpy inside.

Akin to this is the fallacy of *False Generality* or *Doubtful Precedent*. It consists in carelessly or perversely using bad antecedents when better are available. This applies to such current prejudices as that all Frenchmen are frivolous, all Germans mystical, all Jews dishonest, all Carthaginians faithless, all rich people purseproud, all nobles haughty, and so on. Even if all the Carthaginians we personally knew had proved faithless, our general knowledge of mankind should keep us from inferring that a whole nation should be faithless. The most we should conclude is that *some* Carthaginians are faithless, but we are free to exercise caution in future dealings with members of that race. All these generalities are grounded on this prior argument : 'when a known portion of a class exhibits certain qualities, we are justified in inferring that the whole class possess these qualities'—which is only occasionally true.

The fallacy of *Accident* occurs when the precedent is so defined as not to exclude exceptions, and the case happens to be one of the exceptions. 'What gives pain should be abstained from ; surgical operations give pain ; they should therefore be abstained from.' The painful things that should be universally abstained from are those which give needless or useless pain, not the sort that give less pain than they remove. Falstaff committed this fallacy when he supposed that the King would be a boon companion like the Prince. So did the colonists who introduced rabbits and water-cress into Australia, on the supposition that they would there have the same function or value as in Great Britain. In consequence of the Accidental change the rabbits have developed into a pest, and the water-cress obstructs navigation.

If the applicate is a property of the subject only when the latter is taken collectively, it will not yield a true conclusion when the parts or individuals of the subject are taken separately. All the angles of a triangle are equal to two right angles, but it does not follow that one of them—though it resembles the triangle to some extent—is equal to two right angles. In this instance we should render the meaning clear by saying 'collectively equal,' when no argument follows and no mistake is made. This is called the fallacy of *Division*.

The fallacy of *Composition* is the converse of this. What is true of several singulars may not be true of all of them taken together. Because each of the witnesses in a law case is liable to error, it does not follow that the concurrent testimony of many is not to be credited. (Jevons.)

Circular or *Tautological* theorems (*Petitio Principii* Begging the Question) are a breach of rule 2, section XVIII. This fallacy often consists in proposing as a precedent the case, or information drawn from the case and stated in other words. 'To allow every man an unbounded freedom of speech must always be, on the whole, advantageous to the State; for it is highly conducive to the interests of the Community that each individual should enjoy a liberty perfectly unlimited of expressing his sentiments.' (Whately.)

It is conducive	that each individual should enjoy
It is advantageous	to allow

There may be tautology in a single word—the 'question-begging epithet.' We undertake to prove something, but get no further than the use of metaphors implying the point in dispute. For example, some scientific writers are anxious to promote the belief that animal life is a combination of natural forces—that there is no individual life distinct from cosmic life,—but all their proof consists in calling a man or beast a 'machine,' and calling machines 'creatures.' This might be mistaken for the Substantialist doctrine on the same subject, but the two are radically different. Substantialism asserts that man and nature have *similar* lives — materialism teaches that they have only one life in common, and that the coarse, mindless life of the cosmos as conceived realistically.

Conclusions may be used as precedents before verification, but it is not lawful to assume a hypothetical precedent on the understanding that it is to be proved in the course of the argument, and then use the conclusion so obtained to prove its own precedent. This is also dialectical tautology, but the circle includes two or more theorems. When naturalists tell us that in the struggle for life the fittest only survive, and when asked how we know which are the fittest they reply that the fittest are known by the fact of their surviving, we have a tautological argument.

Animals that survive	are the fittest	Fittest animals	survive
A particular animal has survived	*hence it is the fittest of its species*	This animal is the fittest of its species.	*which is the reason it has survived*

Survival under competitive conditions is first assumed, and from it is deduced the superiority of the existing type of animal; then this inferential superiority is offered to justify the previously imagined competitive survival. The two hypotheses waltz round each other without making any rational advance.

When a book is quoted to prove its own authenticity we have this fallacy; or when the precedent is as unknown as the conclusion,—'Paradise was in Armenia, therefore Gihon is an Asiatic river.'

The academical syllogism as defined—not always as presented—contains two fallacies, one of which is tautology. 'ALL Europeans are white; Caius is a European; therefore he is white.' If, as logicians say, the 'all' is absolute and includes Caius even before he is mentioned, then it is clear that the theorem amounts to saying, 'All Europeans are white, and one of them is Caius.' 'Both the twins are fair-haired; Caius is one of the twins; therefore he is fair-haired':—the pretended conclusion is merely a naming of a part of the precedent. The first of these theorems may be interpreted so as to give a valid conclusion. We are informed that an unknown person called Caius is a European; we are not told, and we do not know, what is the colour of his skin; but because all the Europeans we have known have been white, we infer —pending actual knowledge—that Caius is white. Logicians interpret the syllogism otherwise, for they have a notion that reason should give infallible certainty.

After the precedent has been divided into subject and applicate, the former is sometimes used as applicate and so generates a wrong conclusion. This may be called *Cross Reasoning* or *Diagonal Reasoning* —the fallacy termed by logicians 'Undistributed Middle.'

Manx cats	have no tails
This cat has no tail	*it must be a Manx cat*

De Morgan has this example—'His imbecility of character might have been inferred from his proneness to favourites; for all weak princes have this failing.'

All weak princes	are prone
He was prone	he must have been weak

Statements are sometimes put forward as reasoning which contain no case, either expressed or understood. This will seem hardly credible seeing that the illustration of a case is the purpose of argumentation. Not only does it occur, but a certain form of it is regarded by some logicians as valid reasoning. It is the 'particular' syllogism of the Third Figure.

Socrates was poor;
Socrates was wise.

From these premises no conclusion can be extracted, unless it be the verbal summary—'Socrates was both poor and wise.' But logicians draw from it the dialectic conclusion—

Therefore some men have been poor and wise,
or
Therefore one man has been poor and wise.

Both these conclusions are inadmissible. It is because they are empirically true that we are apt to think their truth depends on the antecedent information. If we wish to extend the qualities of Socrates to 'some men' we must make them a case with 'Socrates is poor and wise' for a precedent, but I fail to see how it is to be done. If we add to the premises, 'One man was Socrates, therefore one man was poor and wise,' we have a tautological fallacy.

J. S. Mill notices a fallacy which amounts to an *Inversion* of the Parallel: the conclusion is known or believed and the truth of the antecedents is inferred backwards.

'People continually think and express themselves as if they believed that the premises cannot be false if the conclusion is true. The truth, or supposed truth, of the inferences which follow from a doctrine, often enables it to find acceptance in spite of gross absurdities in it. How many philosophical systems which had scarcely any intrinsic recommendation have been received by thoughtful men because they were supposed to lend additional support to religion, morality, some favourite view of politics, or some other cherished persuasion; not merely because their wishes were thereby enlisted on its side, but because its leading to what they deemed sound conclusions appeared to them a strong presumption in favour of its truth, though the presumption, when viewed in its true light, amounted only to the absence of that particular evidence of falsehood which would have resulted from its leading by correct inference to something already known to be false.'[1]

The conclusion of an argument may sometimes be left unexpressed. If the antecedents are strong and

[1] *Logic*, 'Fallacies,' c. 6.

the conclusion obvious it weakens the argument to state the conclusion in full, besides reflecting on the capacity of the reader or hearer to draw the conclusion for himself. Hence we find at the end of controversial and indignant writings such expressions as—'Comment is superfluous'—'We leave the reader to draw his own conclusions,'—or simply a point of exclamation is appended.

Sophistical insinuations are suggested in this manner. A train of ideas is laid that generates a conclusion which the speaker is afraid or ashamed to put into words.

The second fault of the syllogism as defined may be called the fallacy of *No Application*. It consists in arranging propositions so as to end in a classification, but no applicate is detached and no rational conclusion is drawn. 'Jones is a Welshman; all Welshmen are Britons; therefore Jones is a Briton.' If in actual thinking it were ever desired to establish by argument that Jones is a Briton, it would be with the object of applying to him some quality connoted by Briton, but the presence of which in Jones is a matter of doubt. This would be a conclusion—but not the mere classification.

Irrelevant Conclusion—the fallacy called by Aristotelians *Ignoratio elenchi*—is an attempt to substitute a better argument for the one proposed, but which proves something which has not been denied, or stigmatises something that has not been asserted. It frequently arises from honest ignorance of the question at issue, as in the objections usually made to the Berkeleyan Substantialism. It can also be used as a weapon of sophistry, by confusing the matter in dispute or diverting attention to side issues. It is irrelevant to the truth of a conclusion to point out that he who now supports it formerly opposed it, or that his conduct is inconsistent with a belief in it. Appeals to passion—to reverence for authority—to popular belief—are instances of this fallacy.

The best protection against Fallacy—next to a thorough knowledge of the matter—is a clear notion of the properties of a valid argument; it is useful however to be able to distinguish and name the faulty theorems one constantly meets in controversial speeches and writings.

ACADEMICAL DIALECTIC

XXXI—ANALOGY

LOGICIANS of Greek inspiration apply the term reasoning or argument to at least eight different intellectual operations, some of them important indeed but only one of them argument. This is Analogy—which receives but little notice from logicians because it does not give certain conclusions. The operations mistaken for argument are:
      Immediate Inference—
      Arithmetical Calculation—
      Geometrical Demonstration—
      Induction—
      Aristotle's Dictum—
      Mediate Comparison—
      Syllogism.

XXXII—IMMEDIATE INFERENCE

Some logicians maintain that it is possible to draw a kind of conclusions from one judgment alone. These pretended conclusions are of two species.

The first is a restatement in different words of the whole or part of the single idea, and it is preceded by 'therefore' to give it the appearance of an argument. 'All men suffer, therefore some men suffer.' 'John is a man, therefore he is a living creature.' 'This weighs that down, therefore it is heavier.' These are all obvious tautologisms. It is not an inference to deny the opposite of what we have asserted, as 'The weather is warm, therefore it is not cold.' The conditional and dilemmatic examples of logicians abound in such 'inferences.' We cannot entirely avoid these locutions, as they give point and clearness to speech, but they are not argument, even when introduced by 'therefore.'

The other species of spurious conclusions arises out of what is technically called Conversion. This is a process permitted in Syllogistic in order to render propositions more explicit. The subject may change places with the predicate, a 'some' may be inserted an 'all' suppressed, or a 'not' may be made to qualify one word instead of another. In all this there must be no change in the meaning of the proposition, and therefore there can be no inference. If the second proposition means something more or different from the first, another premise is unconsciously taken for granted, or the supposed interpretation amounts to interpolation. The reasoner may have inadvertently or sophistically added something to the original datum. Here is an example of inference by conversion—'All cabbages are plants, therefore *some* plants are cabbages.' If it is not understood from the terms of the first proposition that plants are limited to such as are cabbages, the 'some' of the converted proposition is an interpolation supplied from the reasoner's knowledge of the matter. In this case the 'quantification' of plants is not a valid inference from the original information.

XXXIII—ARITHMETICAL CALCULATION

ARITHMETIC is first a manipulation of symbols called 'figures.' There are ten of these, and they are capable of many species of combination, and an indefinite number of individual operations under each species.

Certain rules govern each sort of operation, and when the rules are properly understood and recollected the operations can be performed with absolute certainty. Although the figures have names relating to number, and the problems given for exercise make mention of acres, pounds, tons, miles, and all sorts of concrete objects, the symbolic calculations of books have no necessary relation to real things, numbers, or quantities. They are a purely conventional treatment of arbitrary marks that may mean anything or nothing. That is the arithmetic of the 'schools.' There is no trace of reasoning or argument in it—it is mere rule and recollection.

There is however real Number and there is real Quantity. Number is that quality in which a group of three things (for instance) is seen to differ from a group of four or seven, even when the things are otherwise quite similar. We begin by distinguishing ten primary degrees of this difference, and then consider other degrees as multiples or parts of these primary degrees.

Quantity is degree in size, and is a property quite different from number. But, for convenience, we assume that quantities are all units or fractions of certain standard quantities, and we are thus enabled to use the same terms for both number and quantity.

The names which written language provides for the numerical degrees and their combinations are inconvenient to use, and so a set of symbols was devised exclusively for numerical designation. These are the figures of arithmetic. They are the technical vocabulary of number, and of quantity considered as number.

Number and quantity admit of but two kinds of variation—increase and diminution. These variations can be denoted so correctly by figures, that any combination we first make in figures according to rule can be reproduced in real objects, provided the objects are in other respects possible. The result of this perfection of technical nomenclature is that our study of number and quantity has been transferred from real objects to figures. It has become symbolic and indirect, and most of us never go beyond the symbols; that is, what we call arithmetic is an affair of figures, not of true quantities and numbers. We talk of miles, tons, and pounds sterling, but we do not *think* of miles, tons, and pounds sterling—we think of *figures*. A thousand shillings is to us, when arithmetically stated, '1000s.,' just as it is here represented on paper; we do not think of silver coins, and we could not if we tried imagine a thousand things of any sort. There is in reality an enormous difference between '0001s.' and '1000s.,' but to the arithmetician the only objective difference is one of arrangement in figures.

From these considerations it follows that there are two sciences of number. There is the true science which deals with quantities really seen in objects and imagined in the mind, and an artificial science dealing with figures which have only a historical connection with real quantity. Of the latter, unfortunately, our arithmetical education chiefly consists. We are never taught to distinguish number and size in things by the 'eye,' that is, by reason. The symbolism that was originally intended to assist real arithmetical thought has ended by supplanting it. An ignorant shepherd, bricklayer, or carpenter, who is accustomed to make a rapid estimate of the number of things in a mass, or the area of planking in a log, has a better training in real arithmetical science than some mathematicians. If we are obliged to practise genuine arithmetical thought in engineering, astronomy, and other professions, our scholastic symbolism gets realised to some extent, and is a great assistance in arithmetical estimation. But without this it has no more reference to number and quantity than a musical education, based entirely on the printed or written notation, has to the appreciation of musical sounds. A book arithmetician is in the position of a person thoroughly acquainted with theoretical music, and who can even compose music *according to rule*, but who is unable to distinguish a high note from a low one or harmony from discord in actual sound.

It will thus be seen that it is only in the real arithmetic that reasoning can enter. The judgment in free arithmetical observation is the counting of actual groups and the measurement of actual surfaces, and the argument consists in estimating the number of individuals in other groups, and the size of other surfaces, without counting or measurement. But this exercise never enters into symbolic arithmetic. All the apparent conclusions of book arithmetic are tautological; they consist in repeating in one combination of symbols the whole or part of what has been already given in another combination. It is an exercise in expression—nothing more.

Arithmetical ratio has a resemblance to the rational parallel. $3 : 5 :: 9 : 15$ might be arranged thus—

$$\begin{array}{c|c} 5 & 15 \\ \hline 3 & 9 \end{array}$$

This is not argument, for two reasons. (1) The apparent conclusion is not an effort of rational imagination; it is a figure that can be obtained with infallible certainty by treating the other figures according to a rule, which has only to be recollected and applied. (2) The relation between the left-hand figures and the right-hand figures is not a categorical judgment; it is a form of resemblance, and so it cannot yield a valid conclusion.

XXXIV—GEOMETRICAL DEMONSTRATION

This exercise is regarded by logicians as one of the purest forms of argument. It is nothing more than an aid to a certain kind of perception.

Take, for instance, the fifth proposition of the first book of Euclid—'The angles at the base of an isosceles triangle are equal, and if the equal sides be produced the angles on the other side shall also be equal.' The proposition is accompanied by a diagram of an isosceles triangle with the equal sides already produced, so that the conditional phrasing of the proposition does not mean that the production of the sides, and what results therefrom, are future or possible events which neither Euclid nor anybody else has yet experienced, and the probability of which is an argumentative conclusion.

What the proposition means is this: an isosceles triangle of which the equal sides have been produced, has equal angles on the same side of the base both within and without the triangle. It is an affirmation of what is, not of what we must believe to be for reasons to be given.

The truth of the proposition is seen at once from simple inspection of the diagram. It is an association of properties related in a certain manner. It has many relations which the geometer does not mention in this proposition, but those which he mentions are seen to be correctly described as soon as we direct attention to them. If we have any doubt on the subject we remove it by measuring the angles.

Euclid however does not appeal to the powers of inspection we can exercise in this case, and he ignores our facilities for measurement. He appeals to simpler and easier kinds of perception expressed in his axioms, which he began by assuming we were capable of exercising without demonstration. They constitute what he considers the minimum power of relational perception, which if a man have not he cannot be taught geometry. Euclid also in this proposition refers to the result of a prior demonstration, the relation in which he supposes we have seized. By means of these antecedents he *prompts* our perceptive faculty up to the point of seeing the relations expressed in this proposition. If we saw them without the prompting, the latter is superfluous; if the relations do not stand the test of measurement, the prompting goes for nothing.

All Euclid's demonstrations are of this sort. They are pointings-out of what can be seen by inspection and sufficient attention. He is not bringing a case under a precedent—he is describing relations in things, that may serve as precedents in concrete or applied geometry. The service he performs is that of a connoisseur who points out the beauties of a picture or landscape to a careless or uninterested spectator. Relations are sometimes difficult to see—much more difficult than colours or masses—and there is a legitimate sphere of usefulness for people who point out what others are apt to overlook. There is no prediction in this. We are not asked to conceive anything that is not before us. Geometrical demonstration thus assists perception, but does not imply reasoning. Euclid does not argue—he prompts.

Those who maintain that Euclid is syllogistic do so on the ground that the axioms are generalisations, and that as often as one is cited there occurs the subsumption of an object under a class-notion. That would not be argument; but let us suppose it means bringing a case under a precedent. Then if the axioms be precedents and the demonstration an application of them to new cases, the theorem is a fallacy—a useless argument written to prove a foregone certainty, for the conclusion can be and generally is perfectly known without reference to the demonstration.

It appears to me more true to regard the axioms as the simplest relations, which everybody may be supposed capable of perceiving, and that geometrical demonstration consists in showing that other relations not so apparent are really varieties or combinations of the simpler relations. By using in concert with the axioms the relations already demonstrated, we are enabled to grasp relations that would not have been at all obvious on first beginning the geometrical praxis. Euclid's geometry is thus a series of graduated lessons in a special sort of observation, not a system of deductive arguments.

The educational theory that geometry is exceptionally good training for the reason—apart from its practical utility in mechanics—is thus evidently a mistake. Abstract geometry may induce habits of minute observation and exact definition, but reason nowhere enters into the study. As a rational gymnastic there is nothing better than the game of chess.

XXXV—INDUCTION

THOSE who contend that there is a kind of argument called Inductive different from the Deductive, illustrate their view by some such example as the following:—'This, that, and the other magnet' [that is, all the magnets we know] 'attract iron; therefore all possible magnets attract iron.' They say there is an irresistible compulsion in the mind to draw such a conclusion from information of the kind exemplified, and they contrast that type of thought with a deductive argument like—'All magnets attract iron; this object is a magnet; therefore it attracts iron.' They figure the former as a progress upwards, the latter as a regress downwards.

That is Induction as understood by J. S. Mill and Sir William Hamilton; on this point these philosophers happen to agree.

The first of those arguments is a deduction with the precedent omitted. Expressed in full it amounts to this—'Any relation observed several times to subsist between two classes of objects, and concerning which no exception has ever been observed, may be taken as universal; there is such a relation between known magnets and known iron; therefore it may be regarded as universal.' The precedent is not a mental compulsion, but a result of experience. Induction as above defined is therefore only a species of deductive conclusions.

Most logicians take the word Induction in its etymological sense, as meaning systematic observation carried on with a view to obtaining a general idea of some class of objects; or of establishing a categorical relation between one object or class and another, by eliminating all the alternative correlatives. In neither operation would Induction be argument.

In science a 'perfect induction' is one in which all existing objects of a class, or all objects related in a certain manner, have been perceived, so that there is no other object concerning which a conclusion can be drawn. In such cases, says Mill, there is no induction—only a summary of experience. He evidently regarded the conclusion with respect to unknown cases as the essence of induction, whereas in the scientific sense the induction is the positive content of the idea, or the abstract relation—the unknown cases are ignored, or there may be none. In scientific writings induction sometimes means the *method* of observation rather than the result—the method of correcting inferences by perception, wherever possible.

XXXVI—ARISTOTLE'S DICTUM

THIS is usually put into English thus—'Whatever is affirmed or denied of a class, may be affirmed or denied of any part of that class,' and such an affirmation or denial is supposed to be an act of reason. Archbishop Whately expounds the Dictum in analysing the following theorem — Whatever exhibits marks of design had an intelligent author; the world exhibits marks of design; therefore the world had an intelligent author.

'In the first of these premises,' he says, 'we find it assumed universally of the *class* of "things which exhibit marks of design," that they had an intelligent author; and in the other premise, "the world" is referred to that class as comprehended in it: now it is evident that whatever is said of the whole of a class, may be said of anything comprehended in that class: so that we are thus authorised to say of the world, that "it had an intelligent author." Again, if we examine a syllogism with a negative conclusion, as, *e.g.* "nothing which exhibits marks of design could have been produced by chance; the world exhibits, &c.; therefore the world could not have been produced by chance:" the process of Reasoning will be found to be the same; since it is evident, that whatever is *denied* universally of any class may be denied of anything that is comprehended in that class. On further examination it will be found, that all valid arguments whatever may be easily reduced to such a form as that of the foregoing syllogisms; and that consequently the principle on which they are constructed is the UNIVERSAL PRINCIPLE of Reasoning.'[1]

The examples given by Whately are perfectly valid; the first is a constructive argument in the Sixth Category, the second a stigmatic in the Fifth. I have in several places admitted that the arguments adduced

[1] *Logic*, Book I. § 3.

by syllogists are sometimes correct, the fault complained of being in the mode in which such correct arguments are interpreted. They are interpreted wrongly, and then other theorems are found or made agreeing with the *interpretation*, and the admitted soundness of the first theorems is used to procure acceptance for the second. Things brought under the same definition ought to be essentially alike, but they are not so when the utmost latitude is taken to 'assume' that predicates have properties which they obviously have not.

The objections we make to the Dictum as above interpreted are—(1) that in reasoning the precedent (major premise) need not be a class ; (2) if it is a class, it consists of all *known* things of a similar kind, not of all *possible* things of a similar kind. When interpreted in the latter sense the Dictum becomes dialectically tautological, as has been often observed.

XXXVII—MEDIATE COMPARISON

A FEW pages further on Whately gives a totally different account of reasoning, without being aware of his inconsistency.

'Every syllogism has three, and only three terms: viz. the middle term and the two terms (or extremes, as they are commonly called) of the Conclusion or Question. Of these, first, the subject of the conclusion is called the *minor* term; second, its predicate, the *major* term; and third, the *middle* term, (called by the older logicians "Argumentum") is that with which each of them is separately compared, in order to judge of their agreement or disagreement with each other. If therefore there were two middle terms, the extremes or terms of conclusion not being both compared to the same, could not be conclusively compared to each other.'[1]

Here reasoning is made to consist in comparing two things by reference to a third which both resemble. There is not a word about classification, which is declared just before—in loud capitals—to be the universal principle of reasoning!

On this definition we remark—

(1) Comparison by mediation is untrustworthy, unless the qualities compared be rigidly defined or restricted, as in geometry and the use of standards (XXII). In geometry the only two qualities recognised are figure and magnitude. The axiom of mediate comparison means that things having the same magnitude as a third thing are to be considered equal, though they may have different outlines. But the

[1] *Logic*, Book II. c. 3. § 2.

axiom is liable to be untrue in things of three or more qualities. Add colour. Then a white sphere may resemble a white cube on the one side, and a black sphere on the other, but the white cube does not at all resemble the black sphere. This axiom is therefore inadmissible or at least extremely risky in logic, which treats of things having many qualities.

(2) Comparison, however correctly performed, is never the end, but only a means, of reasoning.

XXXVIII—SYLLOGISM

WE have already had two distinct definitions of syllogism. According to the first it is the application of class-attributes to individuals known to belong to the class; according to the second it is the comparison of two things or terms by reference to a third which both resemble. When we arrive at the chapters in logic books devoted to the exposition of the syllogism in detail, we find that the theorems there discussed do not conform to either of those definitions. The only sort of syllogism that can be 'converted' is one consisting of two classifications, and a conclusion which predicates a classification, as thus—

All Englishmen are Europeans;
John Smith is an Englishman;
therefore John Smith is a European.

Observe the difference between this theorem and that adduced in illustration of the Dictum (XXXVI). In the latter the first premise is a categorical judgment and so therefore is the conclusion; in the theorem just given the first premise is a classification, and the conclusion is necessarily a classification.

We first remark that such an 'argument' is never met with in real spontaneous thinking—it occurs only in logic books. It is manufactured exclusively for Peripatetic consumption. The reason it is not to be found is simple—the conclusion it yields is a classification, and that is not enough for valid argument. In reasoning we may introduce a classification as the *minor premise*—that is, the proposition which brings the case under the precedent—but the applicate is never a general or class idea. It is one or more properties abstracted from the subject (whether the latter be a single object or general idea), and applied to the case. Merely to classify a case and so leave it would answer no rational purpose.

Logicians urge in recommendation of this syllogism that it gives a certain conclusion. The premises being correct, the conclusion is infallibly true.

No doubt it is, for in contemplating a thing we can mentally enter it into all the classes to which it appears to belong, whatever be their generality. Knowing the class European and the individual John Smith, we see at once that the latter is contained in the former, and we can do this without putting him first in the minor class English. It is like saying, 'The pavilion is in the garden, John Smith is in the pavilion, therefore he is in the garden.' Of course he is! The minor premise of a double classification is superfluous. The fact that such conclusions are certain, shows how nugatory they are. We are not certain of anything till it has been experienced. In legitimate reasoning the conclusion is never more than probable. The certainty of these double classifications shows that we are stating what we already know—not imagining an ideal addition to our positive knowledge.

Doctrine of the Predicate. So long as logicians are permitted to fabricate their own examples, all is plain sailing with the syllogism. But they are sometimes obliged to deal with genuine arguments. In this case what they do is to assume that *for logical purposes* every predicate of the precedent—that is, the applicate—is a general or class term. Even when an argument is good they spoil it with a bad theory.

Sir William Hamilton states that up to his time logicians recognised but one type of proposition—that called by him the proposition 'in extension,' which means the classifying of the subject. He announced that he intended to introduce a proposition 'in comprehension,' meaning a judgment in the category of inherence—as for instance, 'man is responsible.' He further said that he recognised a third type of proposition, that concerning 'cause and effect.'

But in the course of working out these logical novelties he seems to have discovered that they were irreconcilable with conversion, and so he dropped them. The judgment in comprehension, he then declared, was to all intents and purposes the same as one in extension, and as to causation—why, a cause is a class, and an effect is an individual belonging to that class![1]

Let us see what is the result of treating applicates as general ideas. Take an example in each of the categories.

'The paper is white.' This means that the paper

---

[1] *Lectures*, iii. pp. 287 and 356. The impossibility of reconciling their definitions and rules to real thinking and argument is the despair of logicians. Most of them take to symbols, which are more accommodating than real experience, having just such properties as their makers choose to put in them. Sir William Hamilton had the courage to declare that a logician might use arguments of a concrete or real form, but that it is not necessary they should agree with real fact. 'The logician has a right to suppose any material impossibility, any material falsity; he takes no account of what is objectively impossible or false, he has a right to assume what premises he please, provided that they do not involve a contradiction in terms.'—*Id.* 322. That means in plain English that a logician may misrepresent matters of fact, if he cannot otherwise establish his theory!

has the property or attribute of whiteness. In logic it is interpreted to mean that paper is an individual of the class *white*. This is wrong, for there is no such class. No sane person would form a class out of salt, snow, milk, china, silver, the moon, and other white things; for though they have a common property it is not the sign of a common human utility.

The confusing a single property with a class is not always owing to exigencies of syllogism. It pervades the writings of most Western metaphysicians, and may be accounted for in this manner.

General ideas and abstract properties or ideas have in common that they are *partial* recognitions of what we perceive (XIV). The partition in each is however made in a different way, and for a different purpose. In generalisation the selection is done almost mechanically. We see many things that have some common relation, function, or utility for us, and we remember only so much of them as appears to be necessary for the recognition of that relation or utility—just so much of the Intellectual experience as has always accompanied the Sentimental experience. The process is very like that of putting a piece of wood or ivory in a turning-lathe, and whittling off all that we do not want. A general idea is the useful core of a multitude of superposed observations, each of which had something irrelevant—

something which it is better to forget. We whittle this off and remember only the core.

Abstraction, on the other hand, is a conscious and deliberate operation from beginning to end. It consists in distinguishing one by one the properties of a thing, and even treating each property as if it had an independent existence. For this exercise it is not necessary to observe many things: we can analyse one alone, though an acquaintance with other cognate objects is sometimes necessary to call our attention to single properties. We need the shock of difference to be able to distinguish well a fine abstraction—the difference between shades of colours, for example. Abstraction is thus a minute attention to individuals, and need not for a moment be confounded with generalisation.

Another cause of the confusion in question can be traced to the use of the verb 'is' to represent both the relation of a thing to the general idea it has contributed to form, and the relation of a single property to the thing in which it inheres. We say 'The man *is* a British subject'—classifying him; we say also 'The man *is* cold'—mentioning one of his attributes. There is no class of cold men, and the two relations have nothing in common. A class does not inhere in a man as cold inheres in him. There is no *object* corresponding to class—it is a conceptual creation.

The ambiguity of 'is' favours the syllogistic doctrine of predication, and there is a rule to the effect that in syllogising propositions, all verbs are to be converted into 'is' (or its conjugates) with a participle or noun, so that if they were not before statements of classification they now become such. 'He walks' is clearly no classification; but 'he is walking' is assimilated by false analogy to such a classification as 'he is human,' and so is treated as a classification by those who reason according to the Letter.

The substantive verb has no positive and uniform meaning. As an auxiliary it is a mere sign of tense, and in other positions it is an indefinite mark of relationship, the precise meaning of which must be determined by the subject and the context. It may sometimes be dispensed with in classification, as 'Victoria Regina'—'Phillips, Dentist.'

In the second category we have such propositions as 'the book lies on the table.' In syllogistic this is first altered to 'the book is lying on the table,' and it is feigned that 'lying on the table' is a class or general idea, and 'book' an individual of that class. To interpret 'the groom stands by the horse' a class has to be created, composed of the persons who happen to be standing by horses.

'The mountain is ten miles off' is a judgment in perspective. Syllogistically we are asked to believe that a class of things exists having the common property of being ten miles off, and that the mountain is entered in that class. The absurdity of this doctrine is self-evident.

In the remaining categories the reduction to 'is' has, if possible, a worse effect. In changing 'Canada lies west of Ireland' into 'Canada is a country lying west of Ireland,' we lose the relation in concretion, and express instead a verbal definition. Instead of affirming a position we explain a name. In such a proposition as 'the town of A lies 100 miles due north of B,' it is plain the predicate cannot be a class, for only one place has the quality expressed.

In the fifth category we have such a proposition as 'water freezes when the temperature falls to zero Centigrade.' This is turned into a substantive sentence by saying 'water is that liquid which freezes,' &c., which is a verbal or identical proposition.

'Cecrops founded Athens' is a judgment in causation. In turning it into 'Cecrops was (or is) the founder of Athens,' we emphasise the man's name, but the relation signified by 'founded' is slurred over or lost sight of. Boole converts 'Caesar conquered the Gauls' into 'Caesar is he who conquered the Gauls,'[1] and this he interpreted as classification. We need not be surprised that he should suppose a class could be formed by one individual, for he elsewhere tells us that *Nothing* is a class.[2]

[1] *Laws of Thought*, p. 35.   [2] *Ibid.* p. 47.

Classification is not judgment of any sort—it is a variety of recollection. Logicians imagine it is the only judgment, and so far as they can they degrade true judgments to that spurious form.

Moods of the Syllogism. Having persuaded themselves that classification is the beginning, middle, and end of reasoning, logicians next proceed to divide the matter of their science.

Modern logicians who have some acquaintance with real thinking as exemplified in works of physical science, can, if acting according to their natural intelligence, lay down correct rules for dividing a subject. These are simple and obvious: divide according to fundamental resemblance—let each division correspond to some definite human utility—let the more important properties take precedence of the less important, and so forth: the merest common sense.

But in the division of their own subject they follow Aristotle, and so lose their way.

It is plain that an act of reasoning is a mental thing in the first place, and only when uttered, and thus in a secondary sense, is it a material object. The classification of arguments should therefore follow mental characteristics. Logicians make it follow the material characteristics of the terms in which the arguments are uttered. Their moods of the syllogism are mere varieties of expression, not varieties of reason.

The number of these moods is accidental, depending on flexibility of language and ingenuity in inventing varieties of syntax. Mere transposition of premises constitutes a difference of mood. Logicians however pretend to base their numeration on a more general necessity. They calculate from the distinctive parts of the three propositions forming a syllogism, varied by negation, &c., that there *ought to be* sixty-four moods. Experience proves that in spite of their free and easy method of multiplying syllogistic varieties they cannot produce anything like that number. One logician has thirty-six moods, another thirty-two, a third eleven; the more orthodox fix the number at nineteen. But they all admit that every argument can be reduced to one of four fundamental types—the moods of the First Figure. Why then have more classes than these four? Because, says Whately, it would be 'occasionally tedious' to reduce every argument to the first figure.

If the 11, 19, 32, or 36 classes were natural arguments taken down untouched from men's lips, and it was found to be useless and troublesome to reduce them to four artificial forms, the plea might be admitted. But the so-called valid syllogisms are themselves artificial, and just as tedious to make as the moods of the first figure. Not only so, but an elaborate system of mnemonic rules is provided for reducing the valid moods to the fundamental moods, thus admitting that the former are only intermediate halting places between the natural speech and the fundamental moods. It is *expected* that the intermediates should be reduced to the first figure.

Is there anything analogous to this sort of division in any science or branch of practical thought? Would logicians themselves sanction such a classification in a natural science? If a zoologist, for example, were to determine beforehand how many classes of animals there ought to be, would they not say he was acting improperly? If, after discovering that he had five times as many classes as he could find animals to put into them, he still retained his classification and required his pupils to write out the names or symbols of all the useless classes—would not logicians be apt to call him a pedant? Yet in a modern work on logic such a task is prescribed for students:—

'Write out the sixty-four moods of the syllogism, *and strike out the fifty-three invalid ones.*'

We might have excused the existence of a merely verbal classification in logic, if it were accompanied by and subordinated to a classification of theorems considered as mental facts. But in syllogistic the verbal is the dominant classification, and we have seen from the procedure of Sir William Hamilton—in dropping his categorical judgments—that when the two principles of division conflict, it is the mental which has to give way. The Letter is allowed to kill the Spirit.

All the Moods reducible to One. Syllogists appear not to know their own schematism very well. They say there are four ultimate moods, which it is impossible to reduce to any lower number. But since each of the four is, mentally, a double classification, it must be possible to reflect this common property in the mode of expression. The difference between them can only be verbal. Let us adopt another than the ordinary symbolism.

Cut a card into three triangular pieces of unequal size, and call them by the letters A, B, C, beginning with the largest. These are the terms of the syllogism.

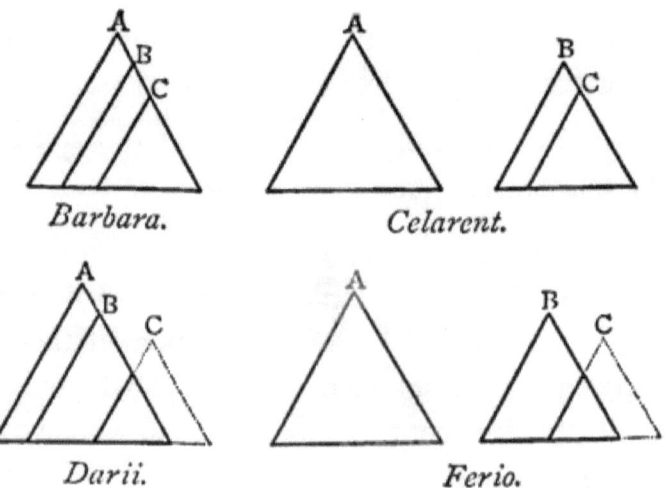

Barbara.   Celarent.

Darii.   Ferio.

The first mood *Barbara* is formed by placing the cards on top of each other, so that B is within the margin of A, and C within the margin of B. This is the syllogism, 'All B is A, all C is B, therefore all C is A.'

Next let B and C be as above, but let A be wholly apart from both. This is *Celarent*: 'No B is A, all C is B, therefore no C is A.'

In *Darii* the whole of B is in A, but only a part of C coincides with B. The syllogism is: 'All B is A, some C is B, therefore some C is A.'

In *Ferio* A is again wholly separated from the others, and C is only partially in B. Argument: 'No B is A, some C is B, therefore some C is not A.'

It is to be remembered that all the other figures and moods are reducible to the above figure of four moods, so that the reduction applicable to the latter is equally applicable to the former.

To reduce *Darii* to *Barbara* all that is necessary is to ignore the dotted part of C. That is suggested by the use of the word 'some,' which has a correlative 'all' or 'others.' But the correlative quantity does not enter into the syllogism, and we know nothing about it. It may not even exist. We are therefore at liberty to substitute for 'some C' the name D, and consider it an integer instead of a fraction. Then we have the *Barbara* syllogism: 'All B is A, all D (= some C) is B, therefore all D is A.' The phrase 'all of some' is quite allowable: 'I met some firemen, all of whom wore brass helmets.'

Ferio in the same manner is reduced to *Celarent*. The dotted part of C is cut away, and the part really significant in the syllogism is called E. Then 'No B is A, all E is B, no E is A.'

Finally *Celarent* can be reduced to *Barbara*. B cannot indeed be enclosed in A, but we assume the existence of a whole having all the characters which A has *not*, or having none of the characters which A has. This is the whole F = Not-A. Then *Celarent* becomes *Barbara* thus: ' All B is F, all C is B, therefore all C is F.'

This demonstrates that there is only one fundamental operation where syllogists suppose there are at least four. The difference is wholly a matter of language, and disappears on changing the names of the terms and ignoring irrelevant suggestions. But the syllogism, I repeat, does not represent the act of reasoning, and its moods and figures are fit only to be a game for children.

STUDIES IN DIALECTIC

XXXIX

THE theorems given for practice in logic books are useful dialectic material, but they do not fully illustrate all the categories. Logicians have no definite categories, and in selecting examples they are unconsciously biassed in favour of those that can be most easily interpreted to signify classification. The really generalistic examples are rare; the most are judgments of inherence, admitted in virtue of the assumption that inherent properties can—when it is needful to preserve the traditional notion of predication—be considered class-ideas. Theorems in perspection and concretion we do not expect to find in logic books, for these, in so far as they are distinct from association, are categories peculiar to the Berkeleyan philosophy.

Whately has the following example in association—'Lias lies above red sandstone; red sandstone lies above coal; therefore lias lies above coal.' No doubt Whately would, in syllogising this, have changed the propositions to 'Red sandstone is lying,' &c., and have assumed that 'lying above coal' is a class to which red sandstone belongs.

∴

Here are examples of arguments in inherence—

A hot skin, quick pulse, intense thirst have invariably in my experience coexisted with fever; the person now examined exhibits these symptoms, so I infer that he has a fever.

Great width of skull between the ears is invariably found united with a destructive temperament; this animal's skull is very wide between the ears; hence it may be concluded that he has a destructive temperament.

Cloven feet belong universally—*i.e.* as far as our experience goes—to horned animals; we may conclude that this fossil animal, since it appears to have had cloven feet, was horned.

I.

Cloven feet	inhere with horns
Fossil animal appears to have had cloven feet	*it is probable he had horns*

∴

When an architect, contemplating the fragments of a building, restores it in imagination after the analogy of similar buildings, we have an argument in inherence. Such speculations are generally too long and complex for analysis, but an instructive example occurs in Canon Rawlinson's *Seventh Oriental Monarchy*, which I will venture to quote, marking the phrases that introduce or express the rational idea. Observe the difference of style between this, which is real practical reasoning, and the trivial certainties of Syllogistic.

'What remains of this massive erection [the Takht-i-Khosru, or palace of Chosroës Anushirwan, at Ctesiphon] is a mere fragment, which, *to judge from the other extant Sassanian ruins*, cannot have formed so much as one fourth part of the original edifice. Nothing has come down to our day but a single vaulted hall on the grandest scale, together with the mere outer wall of what no doubt constituted the main facade of the building. The apartments, which, *according to all analogy*, must have existed at the two sides, and in the rear, of the great hall, some of which *should* have been vaulted, have wholly perished. *Imagination may supply* them from the Firuzabad, or the Mashita palace; but not a trace, even of their foundations, is extant; and the details consequently are uncertain, though the general plan can scarcely be doubted. At each side of the great hall *were probably* two lateral ones, communicating with each other, and capable of being entered either from the hall or from the outer air. Beyond the great hall *was probably* a domed chamber equalling it in width, and opening upon a court, round which were a number of moderate-sized apartments. The entire building *was no doubt* an oblong square, of which the shorter sides seem to have measured 370 feet. It had at least three, and *may not improbably have had* a larger number of entrances, since it belongs to tranquil times and a secure locality.'

∴

The most notable argument in the category of concretion is undoubtedly the inference as to the sphericity of the earth. Next is the sub-inference by Columbus that China could be reached by sailing westward from Portugal. If the syllogistic opinion were valid—that a conclusion must be absolutely true or absolutely false—the expedition of Columbus was based on a fallacy. Most people think it was eminently rational.

No one has seen the north or the south poles, and the conviction that they could be realised, if certain difficulties of transport were overcome, is a sub inference of the same character.

Here is a common type of inference in perspection—

III.

That church	is 100 yards off
A man appears on the roof of the ch.	*he is* 100 *ys. off*

And this—

III.

That distant house	is 60 ft. high
It appears to be scaffolded to a third of its height	*the scaffold is about 20 feet high*

In these cases we have not seen the man or the scaffolding before, and have not measured the latter or the distance to the former: the conclusions are imaginary judgments fairly drawn from known premises.

∴

The deciphering of hieroglyphics, cuneiform inscriptions, and remains of other dead and forgotten languages, is argument in causation. Examples cannot conveniently be quoted even in a condensed form, but this kind of reasoning is most interesting dialectically from the slightness of the analogies that are nevertheless found to give valid conclusions.

∴

This is considered argument by Whately—

I.

Louis	is a good king
The governor of France is Louis	*therefore the g. of F. is a good king*

The supposed case is a verbal proposition, serving to rename the subject of precedent. There is no reasoning. If we already know that Louis is a good king and is also the governor of France (the given matters

P

of fact), there is no rational imagination involved in rearranging these data as in the proposed conclusion.

∴

'He who calls you a man speaks truly; he who calls you a fool calls you a man; therefore he who calls you a fool speaks truly.'—A fallacy of cross reasoning, and the predicate is a class.

All fools	are men
You are a man	*N. C.*

∴

'Nothing is heavier than platina; feathers are heavier than nothing; therefore feathers are heavier than platina.'—A trivial equivoque.

The following is more subtle. 'Theft is a crime; theft was encouraged by the laws of Sparta; therefore the laws of Sparta encouraged crime.'—At most the laws of Sparta encouraged one crime; but there is a fallacy of equivocation. Taking things surreptitiously from the person in whose possession they may be, is not a crime—is not theft—in a society so communistic as the Spartan. There it was encouraged as an exercise in adroitness. This example shows the necessity of knowing the matter of the argument.

∴

'Warm countries alone produce wine; Spain is a warm country; therefore Spain produces wine.'

V.

Wine	is p. in w. countries
Spain is a warm c.	N. C.

∴

'Meat and drink are necessaries of life; the revenues of Vitellius were spent in meat and drink; therefore the revenues of Vitellius were spent on the necessaries of life.'—Fallacy of composition: meat and drink in moderate quantities are necessaries of one life, but not food of every kind and in excessive quantities.

∴

'He who is most hungry eats most; he who eats least is most hungry; therefore he who eats least eats most.'—A fallacy of accident: he who eats least does not *at the same time* eat most.

∴

'Whatever body is in motion must move either in the place where it is, or in the place where it is not; neither of these is possible; therefore there is no such thing as motion.'—It is an abuse of reason to attempt to disprove matters of fact. The conclusion of an argument being always problematical, it can have no force against actual experience. We experience motion, therefore it cannot be disproved.

∴

'A wise lawgiver must either recognise the rewards and punishments of a future state, or he must be able to appeal to an extraordinary Providence, dispensing them regularly in this life; Moses did not do the former, therefore he must have done the latter'— (Warburton, from Whately).—The reasoner omitted to establish that Moses was a wise lawgiver, so that the precedent does not apply to his case, except by courtesy.

∴

'That man is independent of the caprices of fortune who places his chief happiness in moral and intellectual excellence; a true philosopher is independent of the caprices of fortune; therefore a true philosopher is one who places his chief happiness in moral and intellectual excellence.' An instance of cross reasoning.

I.

He who places	is independent
Philosopher is independent	N. C.

∴

'For those who are bent on cultivating their minds by diligent study, the incitement of academical honours is unnecessary; and for the idle it is ineffectual, for such are indifferent to mental improvement; therefore the incitement of academical honours is either unnecessary or ineffectual.'

A fallacy of doubtful precedent: because two kinds of students are not benefited by the hope of honours it is prematurely concluded that no others exist who may be so benefited.

∴

'He who bears arms at the command of the magistrate does what is lawful for a Christian; the Swiss in the French service, and the British in the American service, bore arms at the command of the magistrate; therefore they did what is lawful for a Christian.'

The conclusion is valid so far as the information given enables us to judge. If we know from other sources that the Swiss and British who are referred to, committed atrocities at the command of the magistrate, the conclusion is a fallacy of accident. In general it is lawful to obey a magistrate, but there may be particular cases when it is not.

∴

'Anyone who is candid will refrain from condemning a book without reading it; some reviewers do not refrain from this; therefore some reviewers are not candid.'—This is cross reasoning and invalid. It is one thing to say that the uncandid do not refrain, and another that all who do not refrain are uncandid. The conclusion is taken from the latter proposition, which is not asserted.

∴

'Everyone desires happiness; virtue is happiness; therefore everyone desires virtue.'

	I.
Whoever desires an effect	desires the cause of that effect
Everyone desires the happiness which is caused by virtue	*everyone desires virtue*

The case is manifestly untrue.

∴

'He who has a confirmed habit of any kind of action exercises no self-denial in the practice of that action; a good man has a confirmed habit of virtue; therefore he who exercises self-denial in the practice of virtue is not a good man.'—(Arist. *Eth.* Bk. II., from Whately.)

VI.			I.
He who has a habit, &c.	exercises no self-denial	He who exercises no self-denial in the practice of virtue	is good
A good man has this habit with respect to virtue	*He exercises no self-denial with respect to virtue*	He who *does* exercise, &c.	*N. C.*

The conclusion drawn is fallacious, the second theorem being based on contrast.

∴

'According to theologians, a man must possess faith to be acceptable to the Deity; now he who believes all the fables of heathen mythology must possess faith; therefore such a one must, according to theologians, be acceptable to the Deity.'

'Faith' is ambiguous, meaning in the precedent,

spiritual aspiration, and in the case ignorant credulity.

∴

'No evil should be allowed that good may come of it; all punishment is an evil; therefore no punishment should be allowed that good may come of it.' —'Evil' is ambiguous, meaning wrong-doing in the precedent and pain in the case; the conclusion is therefore fallacious.

∴

'The principles of justice are variable; the appointments of nature are invariable; therefore the principles of justice are no appointments of nature.'—(Arist. *Eth.* Bk. V., from Whately.) The terms 'principles of justice' and 'nature' require to be defined. It might be said that justice is one principle, everywhere and always the same, and that only its embodiments in law and custom are variable.

∴

'What happens every day is not improbable; some things, against which the chances are many thousands to one, happen every day; therefore some things against which the chances are many thousands to one, are not improbable.'—A fallacy of division: that improbable things in general happen every day does not render the occurrence of any one a probable event.

∴

'Protection from punishment is plainly due to the innocent; therefore, as you maintain that this person ought not to be punished, it appears that you are convinced of his innocence.'—A fallacy of cross reasoning.

I.

Innocent persons	deserve protection
This person deserves protection	*N. C.*

∴

'He who cannot possibly act otherwise than he does, has neither merit nor demerit in his action; a liberal and benevolent man cannot possibly act otherwise than he does in relieving the poor; therefore such a man has neither merit nor demerit in his action.'—To 'have merit in an action' is scarcely intelligible. A man's merit is in his character, and his actions are effects and signs of character.

∴

'All the fish that the net inclosed were an indiscriminate mixture of various kinds; those that were set aside and saved as valuable were fish that the net inclosed; therefore those that were set aside and saved as valuable were an indiscriminate mixture of various kinds.'

An instance of the fallacy of division: what is true of the whole contents of the net is not necessarily true of a portion of the contents.

∴

'A desire to gain by another's loss is a violation of the tenth commandment; all gaming, therefore, since it implies a desire to profit at the expense of another, involves a breach of the tenth commandment.'—A valid argument in inherence.

All desire to gain by, &c.	violates
Gaming involves this kind of desire	*it violates*

∴

'He that destroys a man who usurps despotic power in a free country, deserves well of his countrymen; Brutus destroyed Caesar, who usurped despotic power in Rome; therefore he deserved well of the Romans.'—If Rome was 'a free country' the conclusion is valid.

∴

'No fish suckles its young; the whale suckles its young; the whale is therefore no fish.'

I.

What suckles	is no-fish
Whale suckles	*it is no-fish*

∴

'This explosion must have been occasioned by gunpowder, for nothing else would have possessed sufficient force.'

	V.
Explosions of a certain destructiveness	can only be occasioned by gunpowder
This explosion has that destructiveness	*it must have been occasioned by gunpowder*

∴

'Every man should be moderate, for excess will cause disease.'

	V.
To avoid disease	moderation is requisite
Every man should avoid disease	*every man should be moderate*

∴

'Blessed are the merciful, for they shall obtain mercy.'

	I.
To obtain mercy	is blessed
Those who show mercy obtain mercy	*they must be considered blessed*

∴

'Some speculative men are unworthy of trust; for they are unwise, and no unwise man can be trusted.'

	I.
Unwise men	are not to be trusted
Some speculative men are unwise	*they are not to be trusted*

∴

'No idle person can be a successful writer of history; therefore Hume, Macaulay, Hallam and Grote must have been industrious.'

I.

Successful historians	are not idle persons
Hume and the rest were successful historians	*they cannot have been idle persons*

∴

'Lithium is an element; for it is an alkali-producing substance, which is a metal, which is an element.'—Fallacy of no-application.

Every alk. prod. subst.	is a metal	Every metal	is an element
L. is alk. p. subst.	*it is a metal*	L. is a metal	*it is an element*

∴

'Rational beings are accountable for their actions; brutes not being rational, are therefore exempt from responsibility.'

I.

Rational beings	are accountable
Brutes not rational	*N. C.*

∴

'Whatever tends to withdraw the mind from pursuits of a low nature deserves to be promoted; classical learning does this, since it gives us a taste for intellectual enjoyments; therefore it deserves to be promoted.'

	V.		I.
Whatever gives	tends	Whatever tends	deserves
Learning gives	*it tends*	Learning tends	*it deserves*

∴

'Bacon was a great lawyer and statesman; and as he was also a philosopher, we may infer that any philosopher may be a great lawyer and statesman.'—The theorem infers the general inherence of philosophy with eminence in law and politics, from the single instance of Bacon: it is evidently a fallacy of doubtful precedent.

∴

'Snowdon is the highest mountain in England and Wales. Snowdon is not so high as Ben Nevis. Therefore the highest mountain in England and Wales is not so high as Ben Nevis.'

This means: 'the highest mountain in England and Wales is called Snowdon, and it is not so high as Ben Nevis.' The apparent conclusion merely repeats a part of the information given already. There is no case. The following is a theorem of the same kind—

'Lithium is the lightest metal known. Lithium is the metal indicated by one bright line in the spectrum.

Therefore the lightest metal known is the metal indicated by a spectrum of one bright line.'

∴

'If ye were Abraham's children, ye would do the works of Abraham.'

VI.

Abraham's children	do his works
If ye were his children	*ye would do his works*

∴

'Since all metals are elements, the most rare of all the metals must be the most rare of all the elements.' —There is a suppressed precedent to the effect that the most rare individual of a species must be the most rare of its genus, which may or may not be true.

∴

'All vice is odious; but avarice is a vice; for it makes men slaves; therefore avarice is odious.'

V.		I.	
Whatever enslaves	is a vice	All vice	is odious
Avarice enslaves	*it is a vice*	Avarice is a vice	*it is odious*

∴

'Bucephalus is a horse; a horse is a quadruped; a

quadruped is an animal; an animal is a substance; therefore Bucephalus is a substance.'

All horses	are quads.	Quads.	animals	Animal	substance
Bu. is a h.	*he is q.*	B. is quad.	*he is an.*	Bu. is an.	*he is subst.*

This is what logicians call a *Sorites*. There may be a chain of valid arguments, in which the conclusion of one is precedent or case of the next; but the propositions just quoted do not make an argument, being merely a string of classifications. If we know what Bucephalus and substance mean, we know by perception that Bucephalus is a substance.

∴

'Every being is then happy when it acquires the proper perfection of its nature; and consequently all vital beings are capable of receiving felicity that are capable of arriving at the perfection of their nature.'

I.

Every being that acquires	is happy
All vital beings capable of acquiring	*must be capable of receiving felicity*

This is perilously near tautology; it can be saved only by assuming that 'every being capable of happiness' is a more extensive class than 'all vital beings capable of arriving at the perfection of their nature.'

∴

'The soul's debility is not owing to her lapse into matter; for as this lapse is voluntary, the soul must have sinned prior to her descent.'

VI.

Voluntary lapse	proves prior sin
Soul's lapse is v.	*her debility must have been antecedent to lapse*

∴

Cogito ergo sum.—

I.

Whatever thinks	is
I think	*I must believe that I am*

That we exist is the most certain fact we know: it cannot be strengthened by any argumentation. If we can doubt that we *are*, we can with better reason doubt that we think.

∴

Here is Hamilton's example of a disjunctive syllogism, which he considered a valid argument—'The hope of immortality is either a rational expectation or an illusion; but the hope of immortality is a rational expectation; therefore the hope of immortality is not an illusion.' It is a flagrant tautologism.

∴

'If man be not a morally responsible being, he must want either the power of recognising moral good (as an intelligent agent), or the power of willing it (as a free agent); but man wants neither of these powers; therefore man is a morally responsible being.'

Adopted by Hamilton from Krug and given as valid. It is first a fallacy of contrast, and if amended in this respect it would still be a fallacy of tautology.

I.

If m. lacked certain pp.	he would be irresp.
He does *not* lack these pp.	*N. C.*

∴

'If Aeschines joined in the public rejoicings, he is inconsistent; if he did not, he is unpatriotic; but he either joined, or not, therefore he is either inconsistent or unpatriotic.'—An excellent specimen of logicians' logic: on a par with this—If it is fine weather, I go; if it rains, I stay; it must either rain or be fine, therefore I must either go or stay.

∴

'If the world were eternal, the most useful arts, such as painting, &c. would be of unknown antiquity: and on the same supposition there would be records long prior to the Mosaic; and likewise the sea and land in all parts of the globe might be expected to maintain the same relative situations now as formerly:

but none of these is the fact: therefore the world is not eternal.'

If some things were different from what they are	the w. would be eternal
They are *not* different	N. C.

∴

'If the world existed from eternity, there would be records prior to the Mosaic; and if it were produced by chance, it would not bear marks of design: there are no records prior to the Mosaic, and the world does bear marks of design: therefore it neither existed from eternity, nor is it the work of chance.'

Two theorems are here mixed together, both fallacies of contrast—

Existence of records	would prove the w. etern.
Records do not exist	the w. is non-eternal

Non-existence of marks	wd. pr. w. made by chance
The marks exist	w. was not made by chance

∴

'If this man were wise, he would not speak irreverently of Scripture in jest; and if he were good he would not do so in earnest; but he does it, either in jest or earnest; therefore he is either not wise or not good.'

As it stands this is quite circular, but it might be rendered valid by generalisation :—

VI.

To speak irrev. of Scr. in jest or earnest	indicates that a man is not wise or not good
This man does it	we must infer that *he is not w. or not g.*

∴

'If virtue were a habit worth acquiring, it must ensure either power, or wealth, or honour, or pleasure; but virtue ensures none of these; therefore virtue is not a habit worth attaining.' Fallacy of contrast—

I.

What ensures	is worth
V. does not ensure	*N. C.*

∴

'If men are not likely to be influenced in the performance of a known duty by taking an oath to perform it, the oaths commonly administered are superfluous; if they are likely to be so influenced, everyone should be made to take an oath to behave rightly throughout his life; but one or other must be the case; *therefore* either the oaths commonly administered are superfluous, or everyone should be made to take an oath to behave rightly throughout his life.'—This will be more intelligible if contracted thus: If oaths fail to influence they are superfluous; if they influence they should be obligatory; but they either influence or do not; therefore they are either superfluous or should be obligatory. There is no argument; the alternative conclusions merely repeat the alternative precedents.

∴

'If virtue is voluntary, vice is voluntary; but virtue is voluntary; therefore so is vice.' (Arist. *Eth.* Bk. III. quoted by Whately.) This is a circular way of saying that we believe it to be a fact that vice is voluntary. The argumentative form is probably supposed to give the assertion greater weight than it would have if expressed as a perceptual judgment.

∴

This is valid argument, according to Hamilton— 'If man were suited to live out of society, he would either be a god or a beast; but man is neither a god nor a beast; therefore he is not suited to live out of society.'—It has faults of contrast and tautology.

I.

Only gods and beasts	are suited
Man is neither g. nor b.	*N. C.*

∴

'If iron is impure, it is brittle; but this iron is

impure; therefore it is brittle.'—A valid dogmatic argument.

I.

Impure iron	is brittle
This iron is imp.	*it must be br.*

∴

'If the weather is fine, we shall go into the country; now the weather is fine, therefore we shall go into the country.'—We never get beyond the simple judgment that our going into the country is associated with fine weather.

∴

The following is valid :—'As often as the weather is fine, my brother has a habit of going into the country; if the weather be fine to-morrow I infer that he will go into the country.' Here a particular hypothetical case is illustrated by reference to a general habit.

∴

'As often as the weather is fine my brother goes into the country; if it be not fine to-morrow I conclude that he will not go into the country.'—A fallacy of contrast: we are not informed in the antecedents what the brother does on wet days.

∴

'If there are sharpers in the company we ought not to gamble; but there are no sharpers in the company; therefore we ought to gamble.'

I.

Presence of sh.	forbids to gamble
Absence of sh.	*N. C.*

∴

'Logic as it was cultivated by the schoolmen proved a fruitless study; therefore logic as it is cultivated at the present day must be a fruitless study likewise.'—We must take the conclusion as valid, until we know in what respects modern logic is superior to scholastic logic.

∴

'Few treatises of science convey important truths, without any admixture of error, in a perspicuous and interesting form: therefore though a treatise would deserve much attention which should possess such excellence, it is plain that few treatises of science do deserve much attention.'

This means no more than that treatises of a certain excellence would deserve attention, and that there are few of them. There is no argument.

∴

'Some objects of great beauty answer no other purpose but to gratify the sight: many flowers have great beauty; and many of them accordingly answer no other purpose than to gratify the sight.'

I.

Some obj. which answer	are beautiful
Many flowers are beaut.	*N. C.*

∴

'None but Whites are civilised; the ancient Germans were Whites; therefore they were civilised.'

I.

All civilised nations	are Whites
Anc. Ger. were Wh.	*N. C.*

∴

'Wilkes was a favourite with the populace; he who is a favourite with the populace must understand how to manage them; he who understands how to manage them must be well acquainted with their character; he who is well acquainted with their character must hold them in contempt; therefore Wilkes must have held the populace in contempt.'

Favourites	must kn. how to manage	He who kn. how to manage	must be acquainted
W. was a fav.	*he knew how to man.*	W. knew	*he was acq.*
He who is acq.	must despise		
W. was acq.	*he must have desp.*		

∴

'Something has existed from eternity. For since

something now is, it is manifest that something always was. Otherwise the things that now are must have risen out of nothing, absolutely and without cause. Which is a plain contradiction in terms. For to say a thing is produced, and yet that there is no cause at all of that production, is to say that something is effected when it is effected by nothing, that is, at the same time when it is not effected at all. Whatever exists has a cause of its existence, either in the necessity of its own nature, and then it must have been of itself eternal: or in the will of some other being, and then that other being must, at least in the order of nature and causality, have existed before it.'

In this theorem we have a case—'Something is'; and a conclusion—'Something has existed from eternity.' The reasoner seeks a credible or conceivable precedent by which to connect that conclusion with the case.

We are offered a choice of two theorems. The first is untenable, for we have never had the experience that is given as precedent; it is also tautological, as the 'something' of the case is the 'whatever' of the precedent.

V.

Whatever exists in the necessity of its own nature	has existed from eternity
'Something' exists in the necessity of its own nature	*it has existed from eternity*

It is not inconceivable that something should be

self-existent, but we know nothing as to its being eternal. We are not familiar enough with self-existent things and eternal things to warrant us in asserting dogmatically that where the first quality is, there also must be the second.

The next theorem is that everything must be caused, and that causation involves a *regressum ad infinitum*. On this principle there must have been things for an eternity backwards. According to the theory of causation given in section XXVII, a true beginning is reached when we discover the motive, design and power that produced an effect. It is not necessary to ask next what caused that motive, design and power. The infinite regress is applicable only to *material sequence*, in which there is no proper beginning or end. The author of the above argument seems to be trying to combine the notion of causation by *will* with that of infinite regress. But his language is too obscure to make it certain what he means exactly.

. · .

The three following theorems—in a diluted form—occur in an otherwise excellent work on the politics and social life of the ancient Greeks.

'The Athenians who opposed the union of Greece and Macedonia were old men, and the result was mischievous; other similar instances are found in history; therefore the government of old men is always mischievous.'—A fallacy of false generality. Everybody knows that some old men have been wise governors. Cicero, from his experience, drew the opposite conclusion—that the only safe rulers were old men.

'All old political leaders are mischievous; Gladstone is old; therefore he is to be considered politically mischievous.'—Even were the precedent not false the argument is superfluous, for the effect of Gladstone's politics is now matter of fact or history.

'Gladstone is politically mischievous; he advocates Home Rule for Ireland; therefore Irish Home Rule must be mischievous.'—A fallacy of division: a political leader might on the whole be mischievous, but his measures need not on that account be each and every one mischievous.

If dialectic were taught generally and on a rational method, a responsible author would avoid bad reasoning of this sort as carefully as he avoids bad grammar, vulgar imagery, or faulty arithmetic.

END